INVEST *in* GOD'S MONEY

It has never happened before in History
Money is invested in Money

R.S. VIJAYARATHINAM

Copyright © R.S. Vijayarathinam 2024
All Rights Reserved.

ISBN 979-8-89498-387-5

This book honors those who have remained steadfast through economic turmoil. It is with a heavy heart that I acknowledge the often-missed plight of the victims.

To my father, R. Sivasankaran, and my mother, S. Malaiammal,
who taught me a treasure greater than gold—love

To my dear boys, Sivaguhan and Sivajohan:
The honour of being your "Dad" is a gift beyond
any monetary value.

And especially to my beloved Shanthi,
my best friend, life partner, and love, may we continue our
joyous journey towards a lifetime of happiness.

Disclaimer

This book is intended only for educational purposes; I do not endorse or promote any product. Any investment made by my advice are subject to market risk. I am not a Sebi registered adviser, hence take advice from a Sebi registered adviser before investing.

Currency Rhyme

Government, Government
Yes, People?
Printing Currency?
No, people!
Telling lies?
No, people!
Open your currency basket.
Ha, ha, ha!

Protect Your Family

Protect your family from Inflation, Hyperinflation and Deflation.

Contents

Financial Knowledge and Intelligence

It's all about connecting the dots.

Friends! Have you ever wondered about the connection between money smarts and intelligence? Some folks might think that being good with money requires being super bright, but that's not always true. Here will explore the difference between financial know-how and intelligence and why both are important in creating a stable financial future.

Money Knowledge is Accessible to All

Financial knowledge is understanding how money works, like investing, saving, and managing debt. Sure, some people might have a knack for money, but most of us can learn about finances.

Many resources are available to help us, like books, online classes, and even talking to a financial adviser.

And the good news is, even if you don't think you're naturally great with money, you can still become a pro with some dedication and hard work. No matter where you're starting, there's always room to grow and improve.

Intelligence Matters Too

On the other hand, intelligence refers to learning, understanding, and applying knowledge and skills. While intelligence can play a role in finance, it's not the only thing that counts. Motivation, discipline, and determination are crucial in creating a solid financial future.

Intelligence can differ for each person, and it's tough to measure. Some people might be super bright in one area but not so much in another. Similarly, someone smart in one way might need to learn more about finances and vice versa.

Why You Need Both

Financial knowledge and intelligence are the best way to succeed with your money. With financial knowledge, you'll understand the basics of managing your finances and making intelligent decisions. And with intelligence, you'll be able to apply that knowledge creatively, finding new and better ways to handle your money.

Introduction

Understanding the Importance of Protecting Your Purchasing Power

My sincerest hope for you is that this book alters your perspective, making you prosperous during the challenging years to come.

Protecting your purchasing power is one of the most crucial things to consider when managing your finances. After all, if money doesn't retain its worth over time, what good is it to have it??

Unfortunately, due to various economic factors, such as **inflation**, currency fluctuations, and market instability, the value of money can constantly change. Here, purchasing power becomes essential. The number of products or services one unit of money can purchase is its purchasing power. The more you can buy with the same amount of money, the greater your purchasing power.

Imagine, if you had 100 currency note in the year 2000, you could buy more goods and services than you could today with that same 100 currency note. Because of **inflation**, your money has decreased over time due to rising costs for products and services. That's why protecting your purchasing power is essential for maintaining your standard of living and achieving financial stability.

Unfortunately, traditional investment options, such as stocks, bonds, and even real estate, are often insufficient to protect against **inflation**. These options can be risky and may need to perform better in certain economic conditions. Investing in natural silver and gold comes in. These precious metals have been used as a store of value for thousands of years to protect purchasing power.

In this book, we will explore the history of money and how it relates to purchasing power, the dangers of traditional investment options, and the benefits of investing in natural silver and gold. We will also provide guidance on effectively investing in genuine silver and gold, navigating the silver and gold markets, and protecting and storing your investments. By the end of my book, you will have the knowledge and tools to take control of your financial future and preserve your purchasing power with real silver and gold.

One thing to remember is that investing in precious metals like silver and gold is not a get-rich-quick; it's a long-term strategy, and it's essential to research and consult with a professional before making any investment decisions. However, if you're ready to learn more about preserving your purchasing power and achieving financial stability, let's get started on this journey together!

Chapter One

Gold/Silver is Money

Gold & Silver is Mother Nature

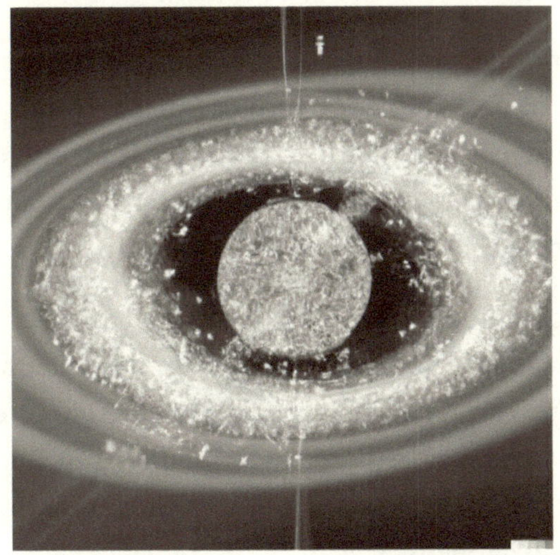

It might be unclear for you to understand how mother nature created gold and silver.

You cannot create gold and silver using a paper printing press or computer technology.

Gold and silver by nature (Not by bank) are produced through a process called "gold nucleosynthesis." This process occurs in stars, specifically in the final stages of their life cycle. When a star runs out of energy, it can no longer generate the energy needed to maintain its internal structure. As a result, the star collapses under its gravity, and the intense pressure and heat cause the nuclei of atoms to fuse. This process creates heavier elements, including gold.

Once the star explodes in a supernova, the newly created elements, including gold, are scattered into space. Over time, these elements can come together to form new celestial bodies, such as planets and asteroids; through the process of asteroid and planet collision, gold and other precious metals nature to the Earth's surface, where they can be mined.

It's important to note that the gold found on Earth is not pure; it's seen as part of gold ore, a mixture of other minerals and metals. The gold that is mined is then extracted from the ore through a process called gold extraction, which can be complicated and time-consuming.

Extracting gold and silver from the Earth can be tricky, but it's definitely doable. The first step is to locate and mine the ore deposits. This can be a challenge, as the ores are often found in remote areas and can be deep underground. But once the ore is mined, it's ready to be transported to a processing facility where the real magic happens.

The extraction process can take a bit of time and effort, but it's possible. One common method used to extract gold and silver is called cyanide leaching. This process involves grinding the ore into a fine powder and mixing it with a cyanide solution. The cyanide reacts with the gold and silver, causing them to separate from the other minerals in the ore. The gold and silver can then be collected.

Another method used to extract gold and silver is smelting. This process involves heating the ore to a high temperature, which causes the gold and silver to melt and separate from the other minerals. This is like a big pot where the metals are separated from the other ingredients.

Once the gold and silver are extracted, they are refined to remove any impurities. This can be tricky, as contaminants can be present in tiny amounts and difficult to detect. But with the right tools and techniques, it's possible to get the gold and silver to a pure state.

Overall, extracting gold and silver from the Earth can be a process, but with the right know-how and patience, it's possible to get these precious metals out of the Earth and ready for use.

2

God's Money

Sambandar (<u>Tamil</u>: சம்பந்தர்), also referred to as Tirugnana Sambandar (Holy Sage Sambandar), was a <u>Shaiva</u> poet-saint of <u>Tamil Nadu</u> who lived sometime in the 7th century CE. He was a child prodigy who lived just 16 years. According to the Tamil Shaiva tradition

At a time when the people of the world were suffering from famine, Sambandar sang this song in the temple of Lord Shiva called Tiruveezhimila, got money (Gold Coin) from the Lord and sold the gold coin (Money), relieved the famine of the people.

வாசி தீரவே, காசு நல்குவீர்
மாசின் மிழலையீர், ஏச லில்லையே

Vassi Theerave, Kaasu Nalguveer
Massin Mizhalaiyeer, aesal-illaiye!

People have been using gold and silver as money for thousands of years because these metals have some unique characteristics that make them perfect for use as currency. For starters, they are both hard to come by, which makes them valuable. This means that people were willing to trade goods and services for a piece of gold or silver, as they knew it was worth something.

Another great thing about gold and silver is that they are incredibly durable. Unlike paper money, which can get torn or wet, gold and silver can last for centuries without breaking down.

This is really important for something that you're using as money because you want your hard-earned savings to stay intact in your pocket!

Gold and silver are also straightforward to divide into smaller pieces. This is handy when buying something that costs less than a real gold or silver coin. You can break off a portion of the gold/silver coin and use that instead. And, because gold/silver has been used as money for so long, everyone knows what they look like, so you don't have to worry about getting tricked by a fake coin.

Finally, gold and silver are just beautiful! People have always been attracted to shiny, yellow metal, and it's easy to understand why. It's a symbol of wealth and prosperity, and it's something that people have always wanted to own. It's no wonder that gold and silver have been in people's hands as money for so many years.

So, those are some of the reasons why people have used gold and silver as money for so long. They're valuable, durable, divisible, easy to recognize, and great-looking. It's hard to beat that combination!

3

Gold Helped Barter System

Let me tell you a little about how gold played a significant role in the development of the barter system.

In the early days of trade, people would exchange goods and services directly. But as societies grew and became more complex, this became less practical. For example, imagine you're a farmer and want to buy new tools from a blacksmith. The problem is the blacksmith doesn't want any of your products (Tomato). He wants some potatoes. So, you have to go and trade your produce for potato with someone who does want it and then take that potato to the blacksmith to buy the tools. It is called the barter system and can be cumbersome and inefficient.

That's where gold comes in. One of the main advantages of gold is that it is universally recognized and accepted as valuable. It means that people from different cultures and regions were willing to trade goods and services for gold, even if they didn't have a direct use for it. It made trade much more efficient, as you didn't have to find someone with the expected product that you had to trade. You could trade for gold and then use that gold to buy what you wanted.

Another advantage of gold is that it is easily divisible and transportable. And made it possible for people to trade small amounts of gold for goods and services rather than having to exchange large, heavy items. Plus, gold doesn't rust, so it can be stored and transported without losing value. It helped to establish gold as a reliable store of value, which further helped to set it as a medium of exchange.

Gold also has a long history of being used as money, which helped to establish trust and confidence in it as a medium of exchange. Because gold has been used as money for so long, people have come to trust it as a reliable store of value. It helped to establish it as a medium of exchange, as people were more likely to accept gold as payment if they knew it had value.

All these factors combined made gold a perfect choice for the barter system. It was universally recognized and accepted as valuable, easily divisible, transportable, durable, and had a long history of being used as money. It made trade more efficient and convenient and helped to establish trust and confidence in the system.

So, gold played a significant role in the development of the barter system by providing a universally recognized and accepted medium of exchange, which made trade more efficient and convenient. Its durability, transportability, and corrosion resistance made it an ideal store of value. And its historical use as money helped to establish trust and confidence in it as a medium of exchange.

4

The Barter System Pros and Cons

Let me explain to you. One form of exchange is the barter system, where goods and services are exchanged directly with one another instead of using money. It's been around for thousands of years and has played an essential role in human history. But like any system, it has its pros and cons.

Let's start with the pros:

- **No need for money:** One of the most significant benefits of the barter system is that it doesn't rely on a common medium of exchange, like money. It can be helpful in situations where money is in short supply or doesn't exist at all.
- **Promotes self-sufficiency:** In a barter economy, people are encouraged to produce goods and services rather than rely on others. It can be a good thing, as it promotes self-sufficiency and can help to build strong communities.
- **Encourages creativity:** When people are trading directly with one another, they must be creative in finding ways to make a deal. It can lead to new and innovative ways of doing things.

Now let's look at the cons:

- **Limited options:** In a barter system, you can only trade goods and services with people who have what you want and want what you have. It can be limiting and make it difficult to get the necessary things.
- **Difficulty in valuing goods and services**: With a common medium of exchange, it can be easier to put a value on goods and services. It can make it difficult to make fair trades.
- **No way to save for the future:** Without a common medium of exchange, it isn't easy to save for the future. It's hard to accumulate wealth or plan for the long term.
- **Can be inefficient**: Bartering can be time-consuming and weak, as people have to find someone who wants what they have and has what they want. It can lead to lost opportunities and wasted resources.

So, as you can see, the barter system has pros and cons. It can be helpful in certain situations, but it also has its limitations. It's essential to understand both the advantages and disadvantages of the barter system to make informed decisions about how to trade and conduct business.

Gold helped the barter system by providing a universally recognized and accepted medium of exchange, which made trade more efficient and convenient.

5

Abandoning Gold as Money

Gold was used as money for thousands of years, but over time, it was eventually abandoned as the primary role of money. There are a few reasons for this.

One reason is that gold is a limited resource. Although gold is abundant enough to create coins, it's still relatively rare, and mining new gold is costly. It means that as economies grew and trade increased, there wasn't enough gold. Governments and banks started to print paper money, which could be created in much larger quantities, making it easier to facilitate trade.

Another reason is that gold could be more practical for everyday transactions. It's heavy and bulky, making it difficult to transport and store. Additionally, it takes a lot of work to divide gold into small denominations, which makes it challenging to use for small purchases. It is one of the reasons why paper money and coin money were introduced.

A third reason is that gold's value fluctuates based on market conditions and mining production. It can be unreliable as a value store, an essential characteristic of money.

Finally, with the advancement of technology and the digital age, paper money and coin money were replaced by electronic money, and gold as a medium of exchange became less common.

So, while gold has played an essential role in the development of money, it was eventually abandoned as the primary role of money due to its limited availability, practicality issues, value fluctuation, and technological advancements.

Another vital factor to consider is that gold could be more flexible regarding monetary policy. Central banks and governments can't control the supply of gold the same way they can with paper money and coin money, making it challenging to stabilize the economy. For example, central banks can lower interest rates during a recession and increase the money supply to stimulate the economy, but they can't do the same with gold.

Additionally, gold could be more efficient as a means of payment in the digital age. Electronic transactions are now the norm, and gold is not easily transferable in electronic form. It has led to the rise of digital currencies and electronic payment systems, which offer faster and more efficient transactions.

Gold has played an essential role in the development of money; it was eventually abandoned as the primary role of money due to its limited availability, practicality issues, value fluctuation, inflexibility in monetary policy, and lack of efficiency in the digital age. It's still valuable as a store of wealth and plays a role in the global economy.

Chapter Two

Paper Money

1

Paper Money Role

Paper money, also known as fiat money, is a currency created and issued by governments. It is not backed by a physical asset, such as silver or gold, and Is regarded as a valid means of exchange due to its legal tender status.

One of the main advantages of paper money is that it is more practical for everyday transactions. It is lightweight, small, and easy to carry, making it much more convenient than gold or other commodities. Additionally, paper money can be printed in various denominations, making it easy to use for small purchases.

Another advantage of paper money is that it allows for more flexibility in monetary policy. Central banks and governments can control the money supply by printing more or less money, which can help stabilize the economy. For example, during a recession, In addition to lowering interest rates, central banks can expand the money supply to stimulate the economy, which is not possible with gold or other commodities.

Paper money allows more efficient transactions, especially in the digital age. With the rise of electronic commerce and digital payment systems, paper money can be easily transferred electronically, making it more convenient and efficient than gold or other commodities.

However, paper money also has its drawbacks. One of the main concerns is that a physical commodity needs to back paper money. Its value is based on the trust in the issuing government and its ability to maintain the currency's value. **Inflation** can occur when too much paper money is printed, decreasing the currency's value.

Another drawback of paper money is that it can be subject to counterfeiting and fraud. Counterfeit money can be created by criminals using advanced printing technology, making it difficult to detect and lead to a loss of confidence in the currency. Governments must spend resources to combat counterfeiting and ensure the money's authenticity.

Paper currency has another drawback, which is that it can be subject to hyperinflation. **Hyperinflation** is a situation where prices for goods and services rise rapidly, and the value of money falls dramatically. It can happen when governments print too much money to finance their expenses, leading to a loss of confidence in the currency and making it difficult for people to plan for the future.

Finally, paper money can also be subject to physical damage, such as fire, water, or wear and tear, making it challenging to use. This is not the case with digital money; it's more durable and can be easily replaced if lost.

Overall, paper money has several advantages, such as practicality, flexibility in monetary policy, and efficient transactions. Still, it has drawbacks, such as **inflation**, trust in the government, counterfeiting, **hyperinflation**, and physical damage. Governments and central banks have to consider these factors when issuing and managing paper money to ensure the stability and reliability of the currency.

2

Invention of Paper Money

The invention of paper money is an exciting story that goes back thousands of years. The origins of paper money can be traced back to China, where the first known use of paper money was recorded around the 7th century AD.

At the time, China faced a metal coin shortage, making it difficult to conduct trade. The government devised a solution by issuing paper money that could be exchanged for metal coins. These paper notes were known as "jiaozi" and were made from a type called "mulberry bark paper." They were issued by the government and were backed by the promise that they could be exchanged for metal coins.

This early form of paper money was used for several centuries in China and was eventually adopted by other countries in the region, such as Japan and Korea. However, it was in the 17th century that paper money began to be widely used in Europe.

The first European paper money was issued by the Swedish government in the 1660s to finance its war efforts. These notes, known as "Stockholms Banco" notes, were backed by the promise that they could be exchanged for metal coins or government bonds.

In the 17th century, the British government began issuing paper money as "banknotes" published by the Bank of England. These banknotes were widely accepted as payment and backed by gold and other precious metals.

The use of paper money spread rapidly throughout Europe. By the 18th century, paper money was widely used in many countries. The invention of the printing press made it easier to produce paper money, and the development of banking systems made it possible to issue paper money on a large scale.

In the United States, paper money was first issued by the colonies in the 17th century, but it was during the Civil War that the Federal government began publishing paper money on a large scale. These notes, known as "Greenbacks," were not backed by gold or silver but were accepted as legal tender.

In the modern era, paper money has evolved into a digital form with the invention of credit cards, debit cards, and digital wallets, but the basic concept of paper money remains the same. It has also dramatically improved the ease and efficiency of financial transactions.

Overall, China is the country where paper money was first created and used in the 7th century AD. The early form of paper money was used for several centuries in China. It was eventually adopted by other countries in the region. It was in the 17th century that paper money began to be widely used in Europe. By the 18th century, it was commonly used in many countries. The invention of the printing press and the development of banking systems made it possible to issue paper money on a large scale.

3

Dangerous Paper Money

Using paper money has many benefits, but it also has some dangerous aspects that must be addressed. These dangers can be both economic and societal, and it's essential to understand them and use paper money responsibly.

One of the biggest dangers of paper money is the potential for **inflation**. When a government or central bank prints too much paper money, it can cause the value of money to decrease. It can lead to higher prices for goods and services and make it more difficult for people to afford the things they need. In extreme cases, hyper**inflation** can occur, where the value of money becomes virtually worthless. It can have devastating effects on an economy and can lead to widespread poverty and social unrest.

Another danger of paper money is the potential for financial bubbles. When paper money is easy to come by, it can lead to speculation and excessive risk-taking. It can lead to financial bubbles, where the prices of assets such as stocks, real estate, and commodities become artificially inflated. When these bubbles burst, it can lead to financial crises and widespread economic hardship.

Another danger of paper money is that it can be used to fund illegal activities. Criminals can use paper money to finance their operations and to launder their proceeds. It can lead to the proliferation of crime and undermine a society's stability and security.

Lastly, paper money can also be used as a tool of oppression by governments. When a government can print large amounts of paper money, it can use this power to control the economy and the population. It can lead to authoritarian regimes and the suppression of individual rights and freedoms.

Another danger of paper money is the potential for monetary policy failures. Central banks and governments can control the circulation of paper money. If they fail to do so responsibly and prudently, it can lead to economic instability. For example, suppose a central bank keeps interest rates too low for too long. In that case, it can lead to the creation of asset bubbles, like the housing bubble in the early 2000s, which can have devastating consequences when they burst. Similarly, a central bank raising interest rates too quickly can cause a recession or depression.

Another potential danger of paper money is the vulnerability to counterfeiting. Although counterfeiting technology has advanced, paper money can still be counterfeited. It can lead to a loss of currency confidence and undermine the economy. In addition, it is crucial to consider the environmental impact of paper money production; it requires resources and energy, and with the increasing use of digital money, the production of paper money can be reduced.

Using paper money can also harm financial inclusion, as only some have equal access to banking services. Therefore, paper money can be used to exclude certain groups of people from the economy. It can lead to greater economic inequality and make it more challenging for underrepresented populations to escape poverty.

Overall, paper money has many benefits, but it also has some dangerous aspects that should not be ignored. Understanding the potential for monetary policy failures, counterfeiting, environmental impact, and financial exclusion caused by paper money is essential. By being aware of these dangers, we can use paper money responsibly and in a way that benefits society as a whole. It's important to consider alternative forms of cash and digital currencies that can mitigate some of the dangers of paper money.

4

Paper Money Fiat Currency

The concept of fiat currency is relatively modern, and It describes paper currency that isn't backed by a tangible good like gold or silver. When paper money becomes fiat currency, it is used as a medium of exchange based on the government's decree that it is legal tender and must be accepted.

The history of fiat currency can be traced back to the early 20th century when governments worldwide began to sever the link between paper money and gold. It was done to give central banks more flexibility in their monetary policy and to help stabilize their economies during times of crisis.

One of the most notable examples of fiat currency is the United States dollar, which was created in 1971 after President Richard Nixon put an end to the dollar's gold convertibility. It allowed the Federal Reserve to print more money to stimulate the economy during times of recession and to help control **inflation**.

When paper money becomes fiat currency, it can be a double-edged sword. On the one hand, it allows central banks to respond quickly to economic shocks and to help stabilize the economy. On the other hand, it can also lead to **inflation** and currency devaluation if not used responsibly.

Another benefit of fiat currency is that it can be more accessible to the population, as it can be printed at a relatively low cost and distributed through banks and other financial institutions. It can increase financial inclusion and make it easier for people to access the economy.

However, there are some risks and downsides to fiat currency as well. One of the biggest dangers is that fiat currency is not backed by physical silver, gold, or real assets, which means its value is based solely on the faith and credit of the government that issues it. It can make it vulnerable to **inflation** and other economic shocks.

Another risk is that fiat currency can be subject to government manipulation and political interference. Governments can print more money to fund their spending, leading to **inflation** and currency devaluation. It may also result in a lack of confidence and trust in the currency and make it more difficult for people to plan for their financial future.

Chapter Three

Fiat Currency

1

Invention of Fiat Currency & Role

The invention of fiat currency can be traced back to the early 20th century when governments worldwide began to sever the link between paper money and gold. It marked a significant shift in how money was used and viewed, and it has profoundly impacted the global economy.

The first fiat currency is said to be the Chinese paper money issued during the Tang Dynasty. However, the concept of fiat currency as we know it today, money that is not backed by a physical asset such as gold or silver but rather by the government's decree that it is legal tender and must be accepted as such, was first implemented in the United States in the 1930s during the Great Depression.

The United States government, under President Franklin D. Roosevelt, had the country go off the gold standard in 1933, which allowed them to print more money to stimulate the economy during the Great Depression. It marked the official beginning of fiat currency in the United States.

Other countries soon followed suit, as many governments worldwide began to sever the link between paper money and gold to gain more flexibility in their monetary policy and to help stabilize their economies during times of crisis.

The invention of fiat currency has been a double-edged sword. On the one hand, it has allowed central banks to respond quickly to economic shocks and to help stabilize the economy. On the other hand, it has also led to **inflation** and the devaluation of the currency if not used responsibly.

The invention of fiat currency also brought new opportunities to financial inclusion, as it can be printed at a relatively low cost and distributed through banks and other financial institutions. It can increase financial inclusion and make it easier for people to access the economy.

However, the invention of fiat currency also brings several risks. One of the dangerous risks is that fiat currency is not backed, which means its value is based solely on the faith and credit of the government that issues it. It can make it vulnerable to **inflation** and other economic shocks.

Another risk is that fiat currency can be subject to government manipulation and political interference. Governments can print more money to fund their spending, leading to **inflation** and currency devaluation. It may also cause people to lose faith in the value of money, which will make it more challenging for them to plan for their financial future.

Another risk associated with the invention of fiat currency is the potential for monetary policy failures. Central banks and governments can control the circulation of fiat currency. If they fail to do so responsibly and prudently, it can lead to economic instability. For example, if a central bank keeps interest rates too low for too long, it can create asset bubbles, like the housing bubble in the early 2000s, which can have devastating consequences when they burst. Similarly, a central bank raising interest rates too quickly can cause a recession or depression.

Additionally, the invention of fiat currency has led to the rise of a debt-based economy. Governments, businesses, and individuals can borrow money more easily, as the fiat currency can be created at will. It can lead to excessive debt levels and put the economy at risk of a financial crisis.

Furthermore, the invention of fiat currency has led to the rise of financial speculation, as people can borrow money to buy assets, like stocks, real estate, and commodities, driving prices up and creating bubbles. It can lead to financial crises and widespread economic hardship.

Another potential danger of fiat currency is the vulnerability to counterfeiting. Although counterfeiting technology has advanced, fiat currency can still be counterfeited. It can lead to losing confidence in the money and undermine the economy.

Overall, the invention of fiat currency has brought many economic benefits, such as flexibility in monetary policy and financial inclusion. Still, there are some dangers that should be addressed.

Central banks and governments must be responsible and prudent in managing the supply of fiat currency and consider the potential risks of monetary policy failures, debt-based economy, financial speculation, counterfeiting, and other threats. With the increasing use of digital currencies and alternative forms of money, it's essential to consider how fiat currency can be used sustainably and responsibly.

2

Fiat Currency No Value

Fiat currency is not backed by a real asset like a gold or silver commodity but rather by the government that issues it. It means that the value of fiat currency is based on trust in the government that gives it rather than the value of a tangible asset.

One of the main arguments against fiat currency is that it has no intrinsic value. It means that the money itself is not worth anything, and its value is solely based on the belief that it can be exchanged for goods and services. It is in contrast to a commodity-backed currency, such as gold, which has value because of the inherent value of the commodity that backs it.

Another argument against fiat currency is that it is subject to **inflation**. Because the government can print more money at any time, there is an inherent risk that the currency's value will decrease over time. It can lead to a decrease in purchasing power, which means that the same amount of money will not be able to buy as much as it could before.

Despite these criticisms, fiat currency is still widely used around the world. The main reason is that it is a convenient and efficient means of exchange. It is easy to carry around and can be used to purchase a wide variety of goods and services. Additionally, many governments have implemented measures to help stabilize the value of their currency, such as central banks that control the money supply.

Overall, while fiat currency may not have intrinsic value and is subject to **inflation**, it is still widely used and accepted as a means of exchange. Being knowledgeable about the dangers and risks associated with fiat currency can still be a convenient and efficient way to conduct transactions.

3

Fiat Currency Loses Its Value

When a fiat currency loses its value, it can have a significant impact on the economy and the people who hold that currency. **Inflation** can become very high, meaning that the cost of goods and services will increase, and the purchasing power of the currency will decrease. This can make it difficult for people to afford basic necessities, such as food and housing. Businesses may also be affected, as they may not be able to sell their goods and services at a profit, leading to a decrease in production and employment.

If a fiat currency becomes worthless, it can also lead to a loss of savings for individuals and businesses. This can be especially difficult for people who have saved their money for a specific purpose, such as retirement or education. Banks and other financial institutions may also be affected, as they may have a large amount of worthless currency on their balance sheets.

In extreme cases, a loss of trust in a fiat currency can lead to hyper**inflation**, where the **inflation** rate becomes so high that the currency becomes practically worthless. This has occurred in several countries throughout history, such as Germany in the 1920s and, more recently, in countries like Venezuela and Zimbabwe. Hyper**inflation** can lead to a complete collapse of the economy, as people lose faith in the currency, and the government may be unable to pay its debts.

To avoid these kinds of consequences, Governments usually take measures to stabilize the value of their currency. Central banks play an important role in controlling the money supply and interest rates, to prevent **inflation** from getting out of control. Government also tries to maintain fiscal discipline, by keeping budget deficit under control and avoid taking on too much debt.

Another important factor that can contribute to a loss of value in fiat currency is political instability or economic mismanagement. If a country is experiencing political turmoil or if the government is not effectively managing the economy, it can lead to a loss of confidence in the currency. This can be especially true in countries that have a history of political or economic instability.

Additionally, fiat currency can also be affected by global economic factors such as currency devaluation. A country's currency can lose value if other countries are experiencing economic growth and their currencies are becoming more valuable in comparison. This can make a country's exports more expensive and less competitive in the global market, leading to a decrease in demand and a loss of value in the currency.

In the event that a fiat currency loses its value, there are several options available for individuals and businesses to protect themselves. One option is to invest in assets that are not tied to the fiat currency, such as gold/silver or real estate. Another option is to invest in a foreign currency or invest in foreign markets. Additionally, some people may choose to use alternative forms of currency, such as cryptocurrencies, which are decentralized and not backed by any government.

Overall, a loss of value in fiat currency can be caused by a variety of factors, including **inflation**, economic mismanagement, political instability, and global economic factors. When a fiat currency loses its value, it can have a significant impact on the economy and the people who hold that currency. Therefore, it's important to be aware of the risks associated with fiat currency and take steps to protect oneself. Governments also play a crucial role in maintaining the trust in their currency by implementing measures to stabilize the value of the currency and maintain fiscal discipline.

4

Impact on Citizen's

When a fiat currency loses its purchasing power, it can significantly impact the citizens who hold that currency. One of the main effects of a loss in purchasing power is **inflation**. As the value of the currency decreases, the cost of goods and services increases, making it more difficult for people to afford necessities. It can be particularly difficult for individuals on fixed incomes, such as retirees or those living in poverty.

Another impact of a loss in purchasing power is a decreased standard of living. People could have to cut back on spending when the price of products and services rises, which would impair their overall quality of life. As more people would find themselves unable to afford basic needs like food, shelter, and healthcare, it might also result in an increase in poverty.

A loss of purchasing power can also lead to a decrease in savings. As the currency's value decreases, savings lose value, making it more difficult for people to plan for the future. It can be complicated for people who have saved for a specific purpose, such as retirement or education.

In addition to these impacts, a loss of purchasing power can also lead to decreased economic activity. Businesses may be unable to sell their products at a profit, leading to reduced production and employment. It can lead to a decline in income and a rise in unemployment, which can further exacerbate the effects of a loss in purchasing power.

To protect themselves against the effects of a loss in purchasing power, individuals can take steps to diversify their assets. Investing in assets not tied to the fiat currency, such as gold or real estate, can help preserve savings and protect against **inflation**. Additionally, investing in foreign currencies or markets helps diversify and protect against a loss in purchasing power.

When a fiat currency loses its purchasing power, it can significantly impact the citizens who hold that currency. One of the main effects of a loss in purchasing power is **inflation**. As the value of the currency decreases, the cost of goods and services increases, making it more difficult for people to afford necessities. It can be particularly difficult for individuals on fixed incomes, such as retirees or those living in poverty.

Another impact of a loss in purchasing power is a decreased standard of living. As the cost of services increases, people may have to cut back on spending, lowering their overall quality of life. It can also lead to increased poverty, as more people may be unable to afford necessities such as food, housing, and healthcare.

A loss of purchasing power can also lead to a decrease in savings. As the currency's value decreases, savings lose value, making it more difficult for people to plan for the future. It can be challenging for people who have saved for a specific purpose, such as retirement or education.

In addition to these impacts, a loss of purchasing power can also lead to decreased economic activity. Businesses may be unable to sell their products at a profit, leading to reduced production and employment. It can lead to a reduction of income and a rise in unemployment, further exacerbating the effects of a loss in purchasing power.

To protect themselves against the effects of a loss in purchasing power, individuals can take steps to diversify their assets. Investing in assets not tied to the fiat currency, such as gold or real estate, can help preserve savings and protect against **inflation**. Additionally, investing in foreign currencies or markets helps diversify and protect against a loss in purchasing power.

Another impact of a loss in purchasing power is that it can increase crime and black market activities. As the currency's value decreases, people may resort to illegal activities to make ends meet. For example, individuals may turn to theft, fraud, or other criminal activities to obtain goods and services they can no longer afford. Black market activities may also increase, as people may turn to unregulated markets to receive goods and services at a lower cost. It can further destabilize the economy and society as a whole.

Furthermore, the loss of purchasing power can also lead to a decrease in investment and long-term economic growth. As the currency's value decreases, investors may be less likely to invest in the country, leading to a decline in economic development. Businesses may also be less likely to invest in new projects or expand their operations, decreasing productivity and innovation.

A loss of purchasing power can also lead to a decrease in international trade and financial transactions. As the currency's value decreases, other countries may be less likely to trade with the government or accept the currency as a means of payment. It can lead to a decline in export and import, which can further impact the economy and citizens.

To mitigate these impacts, governments should address the root causes of a loss in purchasing power and implement policies to control **inflation**, improve economic management and maintain fiscal discipline. They should also take steps to improve the investment environment by implementing procedures to promote economic growth, create jobs, and foster an environment conducive to business and innovation.

Overall, a loss of purchasing power in a fiat currency can significantly impact citizens. It can lead to **inflation**, a decrease in the standard of living, a decrease in savings, and a decrease in economic activity. Therefore, individuals need to be aware of the risks associated with fiat currency and take steps to protect themselves, such as diversifying their assets.

5

Savers of Gold and Silver

When a fiat currency loses its purchasing power, it can significantly impact the economy and the people who hold that currency. One of the ways that individuals and businesses can protect themselves against the effects of a loss in purchasing power is by investing in assets not tied to the fiat currency, such as gold and silver.

Gold and silver, as precious metals, have been used as a store of value for centuries and tend to hold their value well in times of economic uncertainty. As the value of fiat currency decreases, gold and silver may increase, providing a hedge against **inflation** and a loss of purchasing power. When people and businesses invest in gold and silver, they can preserve their wealth and purchasing power, even if the fiat currency loses its value.

Investing in gold and silver can also provide a sense of security during economic turmoil. As the value of fiat currency decreases, gold and silver may increase, providing a stable store of value. Additionally, gold and silver are not dependent on the performance of a single country's economy, as they can be traded globally.

Furthermore, owning physical gold and silver can provide a sense of privacy and anonymity, as these assets are not tied to a person's identity and can be easily transferred and stored. It can be imperative during political or economic instability when people may be concerned about their safety or the safety of their assets.

However, it's important to note that investing in gold and silver also comes with its own set of risks. The price of gold and silver can be affected by various factors, such as global economic conditions, political instability, and supply and demand. Additionally, owning physical gold and silver can be risky, as they can be stolen or lost.

Another advantage of investing in gold and silver is that they can be used as a diversifier in an investment portfolio. A well-diversified portfolio typically includes a mix of assets like real estate as well as alternative investments, such as gold and silver.

Gold and silver can act as a counterbalance to other assets in the portfolio, as their prices tend to move in the opposite direction of other assets, particularly stocks. Gold and silver may perform well when stocks are performing poorly, providing a hedge against losses in other parts of the portfolio. It can reduce overall portfolio risk and increase returns over the long term.

Gold and silver can also act as a store of wealth for long-term investment. They hold their value well over time and can be given down from generation to generation. It makes gold and silver an excellent option for those looking to invest in their children's or grandchildren's future.

Another advantage of investing in gold and silver is that they can be easily traded and converted into cash. Gold and silver can be bought and sold on various markets, such as the stock market, or online platforms, making it easy for investors to liquidate their investments when needed. It can be crucial during economic uncertainty or financial crisis, as investors may need to quickly convert their assets into cash to meet their financial needs.

However, it's important to note that investing in gold and silver also comes with risks. The price of gold and silver can be affected by various factors, such as global economic conditions, political instability, and supply and demand. Additionally, owning physical gold and silver can be risky, as they can be stolen or lost.

Overall, gold and silver owners can hedge against inflation, a loss of purchasing power, and a sense of security and privacy. They can also act as a diversifier in an investment portfolio, a store of wealth for long-term investment, and are easily traded and converted into cash.

6

Impact on Bank Savings Accounts

When a fiat rupee/currency loses its value, it can significantly impact both banks and the individuals who hold savings accounts with those banks.

First, if the value of the fiat rupee/money declines, banks may see a decrease in the value of their assets and an increase in their liabilities. The bank's capital ratios, which gauge a bank's financial soundness, may decline due to this. A bank may be declared insolvent and forced to liquidate or be taken over by authorities if its capital ratios fall below the minimum standards set by regulations. In addition, a collapse in the value of the fiat currency can result in a drop in the value of the bank's loans and a decline in economic activity, which can impact the bank's capacity to make money.

For individuals who hold savings accounts with these banks, a loss of value in the fiat currency can lead to a decrease in the purchasing power of their savings. This means that their savings may not allow them to purchase as much as they could previously. Additionally, individuals may risk losing some or all of their savings if a bank becomes insolvent.

To mitigate these impacts, banks can take steps to diversify their assets and liabilities, such as investing in assets that are not tied to the fiat currency, such as gold or foreign currency. Banks can also improve their risk management practices and strengthen their capital and liquidity positions.

Individuals can also take steps to protect their savings, such as by diversifying their savings across multiple banks and by investing in assets that are not tied to the fiat currency.

Additionally, individuals can stay informed about the financial health of their bank and consider alternative forms of savings, such as savings accounts in a foreign currency. Here most of the foreign currencies are fiat currencies.

Overall, when a fiat currency loses its value, it can significantly impact banks and individuals with savings accounts. Banks can take steps to diversify their assets and liabilities and improve their risk management practices to mitigate these impacts. Individuals can also take steps to protect their savings, such as by diversifying their savings across multiple banks and by investing in assets that are not tied to the fiat currency. It's essential to stay informed and consider all options to protect savings during economic uncertainty.

7

Impact on Share Market

When a fiat currency loses value, it can significantly impact the stock market since the value of businesses and their earnings are frequently associated with the state of the economy and the currency's value.

Firstly, when the currency loses its value, it can lead to a decline in the value of companies and their stock prices. It is because, as the cost of goods and services increases due to **inflation**, companies may not be able to sell their products at a profit, leading to a decrease in production and employment. It can also reduce the company's earnings, leading to a decline in its stock value.

Secondly, a loss of value in the fiat currency can also lead to a decrease in foreign investment. Foreign investors may be less likely to invest in companies or the stock market of a country whose money is losing value. It can lead to a decrease in demand for the country's stocks and stock prices.

Additionally, when the currency loses its value, it can lead to a decline in economic activity, affecting the stock market. As businesses and consumers cut back on spending, companies may see a drop in revenue and earnings, leading to a decrease in stock prices.

To mitigate these impacts, investors can diversify their portfolios and invest in assets not tied to the fiat currency. It can include investing in foreign stocks, bonds, or real estate or investing in gold and silver.

Overall, when a fiat currency loses its value, it can significantly impact the stock market. It can lead to a decline in the value of companies and their stock prices, a decrease in foreign investment, and a reduction in economic activity. Investors can take steps to diversify their portfolios and invest in assets that are not tied to the fiat currency to mitigate these impacts.

8

Impact on Real Estate

For starters, when a currency loses value, the value of real estate falls. As the price of products and services increases due to **inflation**, individuals and businesses may need help to afford the cost of purchasing or renting property. It can reduce demand for real estate, causing property values to fall.

When the Fiat currency loses its value, it can lead to a decline in economic activity, affecting the real estate market. As businesses and consumers cut back on spending, the real estate market may see a decrease in sales and rental activity. It can lead to an increase in vacancies and a reduction in rental and sale prices.

Secondly, a loss of value in the fiat currency can also lead to a decrease in foreign investment, as foreign investors may be less likely to invest in real estate in a country whose Rupee/money is losing value. It can lead to a decrease in demand for the country's real estate and property prices.

Furthermore, when a currency loses its value, it can make it difficult for individuals and businesses to make mortgage or rental payments, leading to an increase in defaults and foreclosures. It can further contribute to a decline in property values.

There is still good news for you; there are ways to protect yourself and your investments during these times. One way is to invest in real estate in areas not directly tied to the currency, such as foreign markets. Additionally, investing in real estate that generates rental income can offset the effects of **inflation** on your investments.

Another way to protect your investments during economic uncertainty is to invest in real estate that generates cash flow, such as rental properties. It provides a steady stream of income that helps offset any potential decline in property values. Additionally, investing in properties in high-demand areas or with solid rental demand can help mitigate the impact of a reduction in property values.

Furthermore, it's essential to be aware of the tax implications of your real estate investments. During economic uncertainty, governments may increase taxes on real estate or introduce new taxes to increase revenue. Awareness of these tax implications and seeking advice from a tax professional can help minimize the impact of these changes on your investments.

Another critical thing to consider is keeping an eye on the mortgage rates because when the currency loses its value, the interest rate can go up, making it harder to afford the mortgage payments. It can lead to an increase in defaults and foreclosures.

Overall, when a fiat currency loses its value, it can significantly impact the real estate market. It's essential to be aware of these potential impacts and take steps to protect your investments. Investing in real estate that generates cash flow or rental income, investing in properties in high-demand areas, and being aware of your real estate investments' tax implications can help mitigate the impact of a decline in property values. Additionally, it's essential to keep an eye on the mortgage rates and seek professional advice to make the best investment decision.

9

Advantages of Gold and Silver

These precious metals have a long history of maintaining their value in times of economic uncertainty and have proven to be a haven for investors.

Firstly, one of the main advantages of investing in gold and silver is that they hedge against **inflation**. As the value of the fiat currency decreases, the value of gold and silver tends to increase, making them a good option for preserving wealth. Gold and silver are considered a store of value, meaning they hold their value for a long time.

Secondly, Investing in gold and silver can also help to diversify an investment portfolio. Investors can reduce overall portfolio risk by investing in assets that are not directly tied to the stock market's performance or the fiat currency.

Thirdly, gold and silver have a low correlation with other assets, which means that they do not tend to move in the same direction as other investments, such as stocks, bonds, and real estate. It can reduce the volatility of an investment portfolio and provide a more stable return.

Furthermore, gold and silver can be easily traded and converted into cash quickly, an essential factor for investors needing access to their funds in the short term.

Overall, If you have gold and silver, it can significantly protect your wealth during economic uncertainty.

Chapter Four

India Rupee

1

Invention of the Indian Rupee

One of the world's first countries to mint coins was India (circa 6th Century BC). Few countries rival India for the sheer diversity of its coinage, be it minting techniques, motifs, sizes, shapes, the metals used, or for that matter, the monetary history arising from the Monetary Standards India has experienced (Tri-metallism, Bi-metallism, the Silver Standard, the Gold Exchange Standard as well as fiat money).

India's independence on August 15, 1947. During the transition period, On August 15, 1950, India released a new distinctive series of coins while retaining its previous monetary system, currency, and coinage.

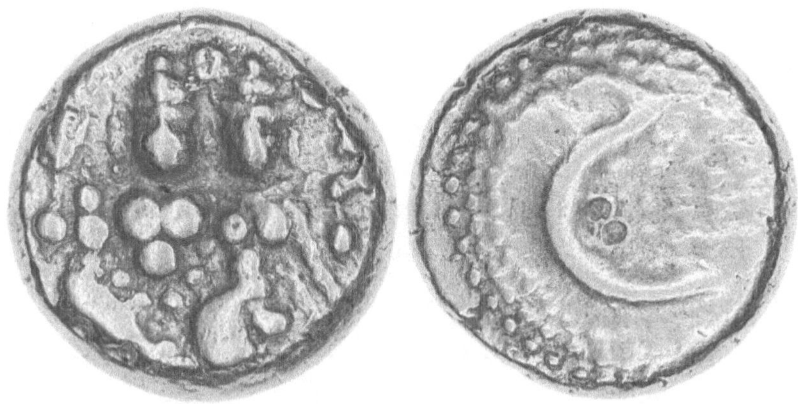

Kingdom of Mysore, Sultan Haidar Ali (1761-1782 AD), Gold Pagoda (3.42g Gold, 11mm).

Side by side figures of Shiva left and Parvati right, each seated, Shiva holds Trishul (trident) in his right hand. Reverse: "HE" in Persian lettering over the granulated field.

The British Raj, the Princely State of Jaisalmer, Silver Rupee dated Regnal Year 22 (1860 AD).

The Sanskrit word "rupya," which implies silver, is the source of the English word "rupee."

Gold and silver coins, primarily punch-marked coins, were used as currency throughout the Maurya and Gupta empires' ancient Indian kingdoms. These coins, widely used throughout the Indian subcontinent, were produced by punching symbols and designs onto metal blanks. I see real money (Gold/Silver) replaced with nickel metal, then became fiat currency.

The rupee was established as a silver coin during the Mughal Empire, which controlled India from the 16th through the 19th centuries. The silver rupee, which the Mughals created, was divided into 180 smaller coins known as "dams." The Mughal rupee was widely used as money across the empire and even outside of it in places like Southeast Asia and the Middle East.

In the 18th century, British colonial rule brought about significant changes to the Indian currency system. The British introduced the gold standard, which pegged the value of the rupee to the value of gold. They also raised paper money from "promissory notes" issued by the East India Company. These "promissory notes" could be redeemed for gold or silver rupees.

In 1947, the Indian government took control of the currency system and introduced a new coin and note series. The new rupee was divided into 100 smaller units called "paise." In 1957, the government introduced a new coin series, which included the one rupee coin made of stainless steel.

In recent years, the Reserve Bank of India has taken steps to modernize the currency system. The government has introduced new security features to prevent counterfeiting, and new coins and notes have been introduced to commemorate important events and personalities.

In recent years, the Reserve Bank of India (RBI) has taken steps to modernize the currency system further. One of the significant changes was the introduction of new security features in the notes and coins to prevent counterfeiting. The RBI has also been working on introducing new technologies to make the currency more secure and efficient.

In 2016, the RBI introduced a new series of notes, starting with the new Rs. 2000 denomination. The new series featured a unique design and new security features. It was made of a new material called "Duraclear." The new Rs. Two thousand notes were smaller in size than the previous notes but had a higher denomination. The new series of rupees also included a picture of Mahatma Gandhi on the front, while several subjects like Indian history, culture, and architecture were depicted on the reverse.

In 2018, the government introduced the new Rs. Two hundred denominations note. The new note was introduced to fill the gap between the Rs. 100 and Rs. 500 notes and to help reduce the burden of carrying too many Rs. 100 notes. The new note was small in size, had a bright yellow color, and featured the portrait of Mahatma Gandhi on the front, and the reverse side featured the theme of 'Rani ki Vav,' an architectural wonder located in Gujarat.

In addition to new notes and coins, the RBI has also been working on introducing new technologies to make the currency more secure and efficient. One of the major initiatives is the implementation of "India's Retail Payment System (IRPS)." The IRPS is a platform that enables the electronic transfer of funds between accounts in a secure, efficient, and cost-effective manner. The platform is expected to help reduce the use of cash and promote digital payments.

Overall, the Indian rupee has come a long way from the ancient punch-marked coins to the modern, secure, and efficient currency we have today. The Indian government and the RBI have been taking steps to modernize the currency system and introduce new notes, coins, and technology.

Rupee Backed by Gold or Silver

The Indian rupee is a fiat currency.

In the past, however, the rupee was pegged to the value of gold and silver. The gold standard, where a country's currency backed by gold, was used in India until the British government took control of the country's monetary system in the late 19th century. After that, the rupee was pegged to the British pound and later to a basket of international currencies.

In the early 20th century, India returned to the gold standard, but it was eventually abandoned in the 1930s as the country struggled with the effects of the Great Depression. Since then, the rupee has been a fiat currency, with its value determined by market forces such as supply and demand.

The rupee is not backed by gold or silver, and the RBI holds a significant amount of gold as part of its reserves. As of 2019, the RBI had 618.2 tons of gold, valued at around $26 billion. This gold is held as a reserve asset and is used to manage the rupee's exchange rate and to meet any unexpected demand for foreign currency.

Recently, discussions and debates have been on whether India should return to the gold standard to back its currency. It would provide a stable value for the rupee and protect it from **inflation**. Others argue that it would limit the government's ability to manage the economy and require more gold to back the currency.

Overall, the Indian rupee is currently a fiat currency. In the past, the rupee was pegged to the value of gold and silver, but it was abandoned in the 1930s.

3

Fiat Rupee (Currency)

You know, now in India, we use the fiat rupee (currency). Let's see what happened to other countries Fiat currency, and you will have an idea of it. Let's have a clear picture of when fiat currency loses its value.

Fiat currency failure has occurred throughout history. One of the earliest known examples of fiat currency failure is from ancient China, where the government would print paper money and then periodically recall it, causing **inflation**.

In more recent history, many countries have experienced hyper**inflation**, which occurs when the money supply increases at an unsustainable rate, leading to a rapid and severe decline in the currency's purchasing power. Examples of hyper**inflation** in history include:

- In the 1920s, the German Mark experienced hyper**inflation** as the government printed large amounts of money to pay for war reparations. Prices rose at an alarming rate, and the currency eventually became worthless.
- In the 1940s, Hungary experienced hyper**inflation** as a result of World War II. Prices rose at a rate of 41% per day, and the currency eventually became worthless.

- In the 1980s, several Latin American countries, such as Argentina and Brazil, experienced hyper**inflation** as a result of poor economic policies and high government spending.
- In the 2000s, Zimbabwe experienced hyper**inflation** as a result of poor economic policies and government corruption. Prices rose at an alarming rate, and the currency eventually became worthless.

Economic collapse can also lead to the failure of a fiat currency. The Great Depression in the 1930s is an example of an economic collapse that affected many countries, leading to a loss of confidence in the currency and a decrease in demand for cash.

War and political instability can also cause fiat currencies to fail. For example, during times of war, governments may print large amounts of money to pay for military expenses, which can lead to hyper**inflation** and the currency's failure. Political instability can also lead to a loss of confidence in money and a decrease in demand.

It's worth noting that some fiat currencies have failed and been replaced by other currencies, while others have died and been replaced by commodity-based currencies, such as gold or silver.

In some cases, currencies have been replaced by a different currency issued by a foreign government. For example, when another country occupies a country, the populated country's currency is replaced by the invader's currency.

In summary, fiat currency failures have occurred throughout history for various reasons, such as **hyperinflation**, economic collapse, war, and political instability. Examples of failed fiat currencies include:

- The German Mark in the 1920s.
- The Hungarian pengo in the 1940s.
- The Zimbabwean dollar in the 2000s.

Some cash has been replaced by other fiat currencies, while commodity-based coins have replaced others.

RBI Creates Fiat Rupee

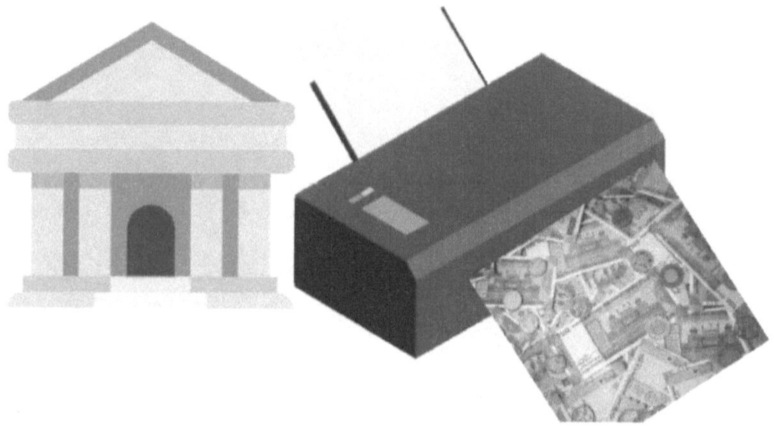

Have you ever wondered how the rupee currency in your pocket gets there? The process of creating and controlling the country's rupee currency is the responsibility of the Reserve Bank of India (RBI). We will look at how the RBI creates money and helps keep our economy running smoothly.

One of the main ways the RBI creates new rupee currency is through "open market operations." When the RBI buys government securities from commercial banks, when the RBI buys these securities, it pays for them with newly created money. This money is then added to the commercial bank's reserves. As a result, banks have more resources, and they can lend more money to the public, which increases the money supply in the economy.

Another way the RBI controls the money supply in the economy is by setting interest rates. Interest rates are the amount of money that banks charge for borrowing money. When the RBI raises interest rates, Banks are forced to borrow money at higher costs, which results in less lending. It can decrease the money supply in the economy. On the other hand, when the RBI lowers interest rates, it becomes cheaper for banks to borrow money, which means they lend more. It can increase the money supply in the economy.

The RBI also plays a vital role in maintaining the currency's integrity in circulation. RBI withdraws old, worn, or counterfeit notes from circulation and replaces them with new cash notes. This process is known as "currency management." The RBI also ensures an adequate supply of notes and coins to meet the public's demand. It ensures that the currency in circulation is in good condition and is easily recognizable.

Overall, the Reserve Bank of India plays a vital role in creating and controlling the country's currency. The RBI creates new money through open market operations and sets interest rates to control the money supply in the economy.

Chapter Five

Gold & Silver Modern Industry Usage

1

Usage of Silver

Silver has been used for centuries in various forms, from coins and jewelry to medical and industrial applications. Silver has become an essential material for a wide range of products and processes in modern industry.

One of the industry's most common uses of silver is in electrical and electronic applications. Silver is an excellent conductor of electricity in manufacturing circuit boards, computer memory, and other electronic components. It is also used in producing solar panels, where its high thermal conductivity allows for efficient heat dissipation.

Another important use of silver in the industry is in medicine. Silver has antimicrobial properties, making it an effective agent in the fight against bacteria, viruses, and other pathogens. It is used in bandages, dressings, and other medical products to prevent infection and promote healing. Silver-based compounds are also used in certain types of antibiotics and wound dressings.

High-quality photographs are created in the world of photography using silver. Images are captured and preserved using silver halide in film and paper. Due to its extremely high reflectivity, silver is utilized to create mirrors and other reflecting surfaces.

Silver is also used to produce jewelry and silverware. Its shine, durability, and resistance to tarnishing make it a popular choice for these items.

In addition, silver is also used in the automotive industry as a catalyst in catalytic converters, which help to reduce harmful emissions from cars.

Silver is a versatile and essential material in modern industry, playing a crucial role in many products and processes. Its unique properties, such as its high conductivity and antimicrobial properties, make it a valuable addition to many different fields, from electronics and medicine to photography and jewelry.

Another critical area of silver in modern industry is water treatment and purification. Silver ions can kill bacteria and other microorganisms, making them an effective method for disinfecting water. It is particularly useful in areas with limited access to clean drinking water. Silver is also used as a coating on water filter systems to prevent bacterial growth.

Silver is used in batteries and fuel cells as a conductor and catalyst in the energy field. Silver is also used in wind turbines, whose high conductivity helps maximize energy output.

Silver is used in textiles, as well as antimicrobial agents in clothing and other fabrics.

Silver-infused fibers can help to prevent the growth of bacteria and odors, making the clothes more hygienic and long-lasting.

In the glass industry, coating the glass increases energy efficiency and reduces solar heat gain.

Silver is used to produce glass, ceramics, and other materials to give them a shiny, reflective finish.

Certain types of pesticides, fungicides, and herbicides are produced due to their ability to kill microorganisms and insects.

In the aerospace industry, silver is used as a coating on aircraft parts to protect them from corrosion and as a reflective surface for insulation.

As we can see, silver has many uses in modern industry, and new applications for metal are constantly being discovered. Its versatility and unique properties make it a valuable material that will continue to play an essential role in many industries.

In the future, silver will be in high demand.

2

Usage of Gold

Gold, also known as the "noble metal," has been used for centuries in various forms, from coins and jewelry to medical and industrial applications. Gold has become an essential material for many products and processes in modern industry.

One of the industry's most common uses of gold is in electrical and electronic applications. Gold is an excellent conductor of electricity in manufacturing circuit boards, computer memory, and other electronic components. Gold connectors are found in many electronic devices, such as smartphones and computers, because of their reliability and durability.

Another important use of gold in the industry is in medicine. Gold has been used for medicinal purposes for centuries due to its non-toxicity and biocompatibility. Gold nanoparticles have been used to deliver drugs to specific body parts, and gold compounds have been used to treat certain types of cancer and other diseases. Gold is also used in dental fillings and crowns, as it is non-toxic and does not cause allergic reactions.

Gold is a popular choice in jewelry and luxury goods due to its attractive yellow color, malleability, and resistance to tarnishing. It is widely used to make rings, bracelets, necklaces, watches, and many other luxury items.

In the aerospace and automotive industry, gold coats parts of aircraft and cars to protect them from corrosion.

In addition, gold is also used in the production of certain types of catalysts, as it helps to increase the efficiency of chemical reactions.

Gold is a versatile and essential material in modern industry, playing a crucial role in many products and processes. Its unique properties, such as its high conductivity, non-toxicity, and biocompatibility, make it a valuable addition to many different fields, from electronics and medicine to jewelry and luxury goods.

Overall, gold is a crucial element in modern industry, and it has a wide range of applications, such as electronic and medical applications, jewelry, aerospace, and the automotive industry. Its unique properties make it a valuable addition to many different fields, and it will continue to be a crucial material in the future.

Chapter Six

Gold & Silver Price Manipulated

1

Silver Price

Like any other commodity, silver is influenced by market factors like supply and demand. However, some investors and analysts think that particular people or organizations, like hedge funds or big banks, control the silver price. It is predicated on the idea that these organizations manipulate the price of silver through massive metal purchases and sales, taking advantage of their access to capital and advantageous market positions.

One of the ways that these entities believed in manipulating the silver market was through short selling. When a buyer borrows shares of a stock or commodity and sells them with the expectation that the price will fall, they can then repurchase the shares at a lower price to send the shares back to the lender and keep the difference. In short, selling can drive down the cost of silver by creating a surplus of the metal on the market, which can lead to a decrease in demand and a drop in the price.

The employment of derivatives is another strategy that is said to be used to influence the silver market. Financial instruments known as derivatives are those whose value is derived from an underlying asset, such as silver. These tools can be used to make significant market positions and wagers on the price of silver. According to some analysts, big banks and hedge funds utilize derivatives to acquire or sell many of these products, thus inflating or deflating the price of silver.

The market could be manipulated through the concentration of ownership. Large banks and hedge funds own a significant amount of silver in the form of ETFs and futures contracts, giving them considerable control over the market. If these entities decide to sell a large number of their silver holdings, it can cause a significant drop in the price of silver.

There have been some reports of manipulation in the silver market. For example, in the late 1970s, it was alleged that the Hunt brothers, 2 wealthy Texas oil company executives, attempted to manipulate the price of silver by buying large amounts of the metal. It caused the price of silver to rise dramatically, ultimately leading to a silver market crash.

Another example was in 2010 when the U.S. Commodity Futures Trading Commission (CFTC) launched an investigation into possible manipulation in the silver market. The research found evidence of manipulation, but the CFTC ultimately concluded that the manipulation was not severe enough to warrant enforcement action.

It's worth noting that while there have been some reports of manipulation in the silver market in the past, it's difficult to prove, and it's also hard to say whether it's still happening in the present or not. The silver market is complex and multifaceted, and many factors can influence the price of silver. Supply and demand are major factors, but it's also essential to consider global economic conditions, geopolitical events, and other factors affecting the market.

Overall, silver prices are subject to market forces such as supply and demand. Still, some investors and analysts believe that specific individuals or groups, such as hedge funds or large banks, manipulate silver's cost. The manipulation theory is based on the belief that these entities use their financial resources and market positions to artificially inflate or deflate the price of silver by buying or selling large.

2

Gold Price

Various factors, including supply and demand, economic conditions, and geopolitical events, determine the price of gold. However, there have been accusations and suspicions that the cost of gold is manipulated by specific individuals or institutions.

One of the main accusations is that large banks and financial institutions manipulate the gold market by short-selling large amounts of gold futures. It creates an artificial supply of gold, which can drive down the price. Some argue that these institutions are incentivized to keep the cost of gold low because it can negatively impact the value of gold mining stocks and other gold-related investments.

Another accusation is that some governments and central banks also manipulate the gold market by buying or selling large amounts of gold. It can also affect the supply and demand and, thus, the price of gold.

There are also accusations of insider trading, where individuals with privileged information about the gold market use that information to make profitable trades.

However, it's important to note that manipulating the price of gold or any other commodity is illegal, and laws and regulations are in place to prevent such activities. Also, it's important to note that there needs to be more concrete evidence to prove that the gold price is manipulated.

Other factors can affect the price of gold, such as changes in interest rates, currency exchange rates, and global economic conditions. These factors can also influence the demand for gold and, thus, its price.

It's also worth noting that gold is considered a haven asset, meaning its price may increase during economic uncertainty and political turmoil.

Overall, while there are accusations and suspicions of gold price manipulation, it's important to remember that many factors can affect the price of gold. It's essential to consider all of them before making any conclusions. It's also important to remember that manipulating the gold market is illegal, and regulations are in place to prevent such activities.

Chapter Seven

Confiscation

1

Gold & Silver Confiscation

India has a long history of using silver and gold as a medium of exchange and store of value. However, there have been instances where the Indian government has implemented policies of confiscation or restriction of private ownership of these precious metals.

One of India's most notable acts of silver and gold confiscation was the Gold Control Act of 1968. This act, implemented by the Indian government, restricted the private ownership of gold and required citizens to turn in their gold to the government in exchange for bonds. The act aimed to curb gold smuggling and reduce the outflow of foreign exchange. The action was criticized for being too restrictive and causing hardship to the people required to turn in their gold.

Another notable act was the Indian government's demonetization in 2016, where the government withdrew the RS 500 and 1000 Rupee notes from circulation. It was done to curb the shadow economy and black money circulation. However, the demonetization caused a lot of hardship to ordinary people, as they were required to deposit their savings in the banks, resulting in a temporary cash shortage.

In addition, the Indian government also implemented gold import restrictions and high import duties to curb gold imports and reduce the current account deficit. These policies are intended to reduce the demand for gold and the outflow of foreign exchange.

It's worth noting that these acts of confiscation or restriction of gold and silver were implemented during economic or political turmoil and intended to support the economy or curb black money. However, they were controversial and may have negative consequences on individuals and the economy.

Overall, while India has a long history of using silver and gold as a medium of exchange and store of value, the Indian government has implemented policies of confiscation or restriction of private ownership of these precious.

It's important to note that these policies are not exclusive to India and have occurred in other countries. It's also important to note that the government implemented these policies intending to address economic issues. Still, they have hurt the citizens and their savings.

Some of the Notable Acts on Silver and Gold Confiscation Around the World:

1. The Gold Reserve Act of 1934 (Executive Order 6814) - This act, signed by President Franklin D. Roosevelt, required all private citizens to turn in their gold to the Federal Reserve in exchange for paper currency. It also authorized the government to devalue the dollar by raising the price of gold.

2. The Silver Purchase Act of 1934 - This act, passed by the U.S. Congress, required the government to purchase a certain amount of silver each month at a fixed price. It was intended to help support the price of silver and stabilize the silver mining industry.

3. The Gold Confiscation of 1933 - President Roosevelt issued an executive order that banned private ownership of gold bullion and required all citizens to turn in their gold to the Federal Reserve in exchange for paper currency.

4. The Silver Confiscation of 1942 - In 1942, the U.S. government seized all privately held silver to support the war effort, paying citizens 41.34 cents per ounce for their silver.

5. The Indian Gold Control Act of 1968 - This act, implemented by the Indian government, restricted the private ownership of gold and required citizens to turn in their gold to the government in exchange for bonds.

6. The Emergency Banking Act of 1933 - This act, passed by the U.S. Congress, authorized the President to prohibit the hoarding of gold and other specified forms of property. It gave the President the power to require individuals to sell their gold to the government at a fixed price.

7. The Gold Reserve Act of 1965 - This act, passed by the U.S. Congress, authorized the U.S. Treasury to sell gold to foreign central banks and authorized the President to impose restrictions on the private ownership of gold.

8. The Comprehensive Anti-Apartheid Act of 1986 - This act, passed by the U.S. Congress, prohibited the export of gold from South Africa and required the U.S. government to divest from companies that did business in South Africa.

9. The Foreign Account Tax Compliance Act (FATCA) - This act, passed by the U.S. Congress in 2010, requires foreign financial institutions to report information

about U.S. citizens who hold accounts with them to the U.S. government. This includes information about gold holdings.

10. Executive Order 6102 - This executive order signed by President Roosevelt in 1933 prohibited the hoarding of gold coins, gold bullion, and gold certificates within the continental United States by individuals, partnerships, associations, and corporations.

11. The National Defense Stockpile Transactions Act of 1999 - This act, passed by the U.S. Congress, authorized the U.S. government to sell silver from the National Defense Stockpile, with the proceeds used to support the Department of Defense.

12. The Dodd-Frank Wall Street Reform & Consumer Protection Act of 2010 - This act, passed by the U.S. Congress, established new regulations for the commodities markets, including the gold and silver markets. It also established the Commodity Futures Trading Commission (CFTC) to oversee and regulate these markets.

13. Act of 1980 Taxing Foreign Investment in Real Property - This act, passed by the U.S. Congress, imposed a withholding tax on the sale of certain types of real property, including gold mines, by foreign investors.

14. The Economic Stabilization Act of 1970 - This act, passed by the U.S. Congress, authorized the President to impose price controls on certain commodities, including gold and silver, in order to stabilize prices and curb **inflation**.

15. The Monetary Control Act of 1980 - This act, passed by the U.S. Congress, authorized the Federal Reserve

to set reserve requirements for depository institutions, including those that hold gold and silver.

16. The Gold Regulations Act of 1864 - This act, passed by the U.S. Congress, authorized the U.S. Treasury to issue gold certificates, which could be used as legal tender and were redeemable for the gold coin. It also prohibited the private ownership of gold bullion and required all citizens to turn in their gold to the government.

17. The Gold Standard Act of 1900 - This act, passed by the U.S. Congress, established gold as the standard for redeeming paper money and established the U.S. gold reserve.

18. The Gold Bullion Coin Act of 1985 - This act, passed by the U.S. Congress, authorized the U.S. Mint to produce gold bullion coins, including the American Eagle gold coin.

19. The Gold Reserve Act of 1934 - This act, passed by the U.S. Congress, authorized the U.S. government to purchase gold from foreign countries, thereby increasing the U.S. gold reserve.

20. The Gold Reserve Act of 1900 - This act, passed by the U.S. Congress, authorized the U.S. government to purchase gold from foreign countries, thereby increasing the U.S. gold reserve.

2

Solution for Gold & Silver Confiscation

When it comes to protecting your investments in gold and silver from confiscation risk, there are a few solutions that investors can consider.

One solution is to hold your gold and silver in a private and secure storage facility, such as a safe deposit or a secret vault. It can provide an added layer of security for your precious metals and make it more difficult for them to be confiscated. Additionally, many private storage facilities are available in countries with strong legal protections for property rights, which can provide an added level of security.

Secondly, investors can consider holding their gold and silver in the form of coins, bars, or ornaments legally tender in their country. It means that they are recognized as money by the government and can be used to purchase goods and services. It can provide an added layer of protection for your precious metals as they are less likely to be confiscated if they are recognized as legal tender.

Thirdly, investors can also consider holding their gold and silver in a foreign country that has a stable political climate and strong legal protections for property rights. It can protect your precious metals as they are less likely to be confiscated if held in a foreign country.

Additionally, investors can consider holding their gold and silver as ETFs (Exchange-Traded Funds) or mining stocks. These options provide exposure to gold and silver without the need for storage or security concerns. It's essential to remember that ETFs and mining stocks carry their own risks, such as fluctuations in the price of gold and silver, and it's essential to do your research before investing in them.

Furthermore, it's crucial to have a well-diversified portfolio that includes a mix of assets such as stocks, bonds, real estate, and cash. It can reduce the overall risk of your portfolio and provide a hedge against confiscation risk. Additionally, it's essential to keep your investments in various forms, such as physical gold and silver, ETFs, mining stocks, and digital assets like Bitcoin. It will help to diversify your risk across different assets and provide a safety net in case one or more of your investments are confiscated.

Another solution is to invest in gold and silver mining companies, which can expose the metal without needing to hold it physically. These companies also have the advantage of producing gold and silver at a lower cost than the current market price, which can provide a hedge against confiscation risk.

It's also essential to stay informed about your country's economic and political climate and have a plan in place in case of confiscation. It can include having a way to quickly and easily convert your precious metals into cash or having a way to quickly and easily move your precious metals to a safe location.

Overall, protecting your investments in gold and silver from confiscation risk requires a well-diversified portfolio and a good understanding of your country's economic and political climate. It also requires certain precautions such as holding your precious metals in private and secure storage facilities, legal tender coins, foreign countries with strong legal protections for property rights, and diversifying your investments across various assets. Additionally, it's crucial to stay informed and have a plan in case of confiscation.

Chapter Eight

World Monetary System

1

World Reserve Currency

The US dollar became the world's primary reserve currency following the Bretton Woods Agreement in 1944. The agreement established the US dollar as the anchor currency for the international monetary system, and other countries pegged the value of their money to the US dollar. It meant that the US dollar was widely used as the primary currency for international trade and as a reserve currency for other countries central banks.

The US dollar's status as the world's reserve currency was solidified after World War II, as the US economy emerged as the strongest in the world, and the US dollar replaced the British pound as the dominant international currency.

Before the US dollar, various currencies are used as the primary international reserve currency. The British pound was widely used as the primary global reserve currency during the 19th century, and the Spanish dollar (also known as the "piece of 8") was widely used as the primary international trade currency during the 18th century.

Before the 18th century, various currencies were used as the primary international trade currency, depending on the region and period. For example, in Europe during the Middle Ages, the Byzantine solidus and the Venetian ducat were widely used as trade currencies. In Asia, the Chinese Yuan and the Indian Rupee were widely used. In the Islamic World, the dinar and the dirham were widely used.

2

Monetary System

Let me show you the different types of monetary systems used throughout history. We'll look at the Gold Standard, the Gold Exchange Standard, the Bretton Woods system, and the current Fiat Currency system. We'll talk about each of these systems and their pros and cons. By this end, you'll better understand how money and economies have evolved. So, let's get started!

India Monetary System: 17th Century:

During the 17th century, India's monetary system was a mixture of different currencies and precious metals. The Mughal Empire used a combination of gold, silver, and copper coins as currency. The gold coins were known as "mohurs," the silver coins were known as "rupayahs," and the copper coins were known as "dam." The Mughal Empire issued these coins, which everyone used as a legal medium of exchange & store of value. The weight and purity of the metal used to make these coins affected their worth.

The authorized Mughal coinage, multiple provincial currencies, and trade practices in various regions of India. The official Mughal coinage, various regional currencies, and business forms in different parts of India. For instance, in some areas, precious metals like gold and silver served as the primary form of exchange, while other types of money, like cowry shells, rice, and salt, served as a secondary form of commerce.

It's worth noting that India's monetary system in the 17th century was not based on any official gold standard system as it was not yet in existence. The currency's value is determined by weight, the fineness of the metal it was made of, and the acceptance of the money by the people.

Gold Standard Monetary System:

100% Gold backed by currency

The Gold Standard is a monetary system in which the currency's value is directly linked to the value of gold. This means that a country's central bank guarantees that a certain amount of cash can be exchanged for a specific amount of gold. It creates a direct relationship between the currency's value and gold's value and helps stabilize the weight. Most developed countries widely used the gold standard in the early 20th century and the late 19th century as a monetary system. Still, it was abandoned by many countries during World War I and later by others during the Great Depression as it limited the ability of governments to use monetary policy to stabilize their economies.

Gold Exchange Monetary System: 1920s - 1930s

50% Gold backed by currency

The Gold Exchange Standard was used between World War I and World War II, approximately from the 1920s to the 1930s. The Gold Exchange Standard was a monetary system where countries pegged the value of their currency to the value of gold and also held reserves of other cash that were also pegged to gold.

Bretton Woods Monetary System: 1944 – 1971

25% Gold backed by currency

At the time of the 1944 establishment of the Bretton Woods system, in which most countries pegged the value of their currency to the US dollar, and the US dollar was bonded to the value of gold. This system was in place until 1971 when the US government suspended the swappable of the dollar to gold due to rising **inflation** and other economic pressures.

Fiat Currency Monetary System: Since 1971, Zero% Gold Backed by Currency

The Fiat Currency Monetary System has been in place since 1971, after the suspension of the convertibility of the US dollar to gold (Temporary) during the Bretton Woods system. It is still used today by most countries around the world.

Future Monetary System:

The monetary system will again go back to the gold standard. If so, what will the fixed gold price be?

Some of Their Pros and Cons

Let's start with the Gold Standard, a monetary system where the value of a currency was directly linked to the value of gold. One of the pros of this system is that it can help stabilize a currency's value. The value of gold is relatively stable. However, it can also be a disadvantage, as the supply of gold is limited and may need help to keep up with the growing needs of the economy. It means the government can only spend what they have.

Next, we have the Gold Exchange Standard. This system is similar to the Gold Standard but allows countries to hold reserves of other currencies pegged to gold. This system's advantage is that allowing users more flexibility in terms of currency reserves. However, it also introduces more complexity, making it more challenging to maintain stable exchange rates.

The Bretton Woods system was where most countries bonded the value of their currency to the US dollar, and the US dollar was bonded to the value of gold. One of the pros of this system was that it helped to promote stability in the international monetary system. However, it also put pressure on the US to maintain the dollar's value at a fixed exchange rate, which proved unsustainable in the long run.

The current fiat currency system is a monetary system where the value of a currency is not linked to the value of any physical commodity but is established by government fiat. One of the pros of this system is that it allows governments to have more flexibility in terms of monetary policy and can help stimulate economic growth. However, it also means that the value of a currency can be more vulnerable to **inflation** and other financial pressures.

3

Monetary System Money Reset

This is a topic that should be discussed more, but it's something that can have a significant impact on a country's economy. Let's examine in more detail what a monetary system money reset is, why it might be necessary, and the potential consequences of such a move. We hope you'll find the information here informative and helpful. So please cross your fingers, and let's get started! Dive in!

Monetary system money reset is a process that can have an impact on a country's economy, and it's something that should be discussed more. We'll take a closer look at what a monetary system money reset is, why it might be necessary, and the potential consequences of such a move.

First, let's define what I mean by a monetary system money reset. Essentially, it's a process of completely overhauling a country's economic system, often replacing the current currency with a new one. This can be done for various reasons, like combating **inflation**, addressing economic problems, or stabilizing money during a financial crisis.

One of the main reasons a country might undertake a monetary system money reset is to combat **inflation**. **Inflation** is when the general level of prices for goods and services is rising. It can be caused by a lot of factors, like an increase in demand for goods and services, an increase in the cost of production, or a decrease in the value of the currency. When **inflation** becomes too high, it can be difficult for people to make ends meet, leading to economic instability. A monetary system money reset can help combat **inflation** by introducing a new currency that is more stable and less prone to **inflation**.

Another reason a country might undertake a monetary system money reset is to address economic problems. For example, suppose a country is experiencing a severe recession. In that case, a financial system money reset can help stimulate economic growth by making it easier for people to borrow money, leading to increased spending and investment.

Finally, a monetary system money reset can stabilize a currency during a financial crisis. During a financial crisis, a country's currency may experience a sharp decline in value, leading to economic instability and a loss of confidence in the government. A monetary system money reset can help stabilize the currency by introducing a new one that is more stable and less prone to fluctuations.

It's worth noting that monetary system money reset is a very complex process and can have significant economic and social consequences. For example, it can lead to confusion and uncertainty among the public and disrupt economic activity. It may also lead to the loss of purchasing power of citizens and a significant change in wealth distribution.

Overall, the monetary system money reset is a process that can significantly impact a country's economy, and this should be discussed in more detail. It can be done for a number of reasons, such as combating **inflation**, addressing economic problems, or stabilizing a currency during a financial crisis. However, it's a complex process with significant economic and social consequences; therefore, it should be carefully considered before implementation.

I hope Gold & Silver will be counted during the money reset, and the price of Lord's money will skyrocket.

Chapter Nine

Depression

1

The Great Depression

Black Tuesday, or the 1929 stock market collapse, marked the start of the Great Depression. On October 29th, the stock market experienced a dramatic drop, with investors selling off their stocks in a panic. This led to a massive decline in stock prices, and many banks and businesses went bankrupt.

The Great Depression's economic collapse was defined by a high unemployment rate, low industrial productivity, and a severe decrease in global trade. In the United States, unemployment reached 25%, and many people could not find work or afford basic necessities. This led to widespread poverty, with many people living in shantytowns and relying on government aid to survive.

The depression also significantly impacted the global economy, with many countries experiencing similar economic problems. The collapse of international trade and the decline in commodity prices led to a decrease in economic activity in many countries.

Governments worldwide tried to combat the depression through various policies and programs. President Franklin D. Roosevelt implemented the New Deal in the United States, a series of programs designed to create jobs and stimulate economic growth. Other countries also implemented protectionism, currency devaluation, and government spending policies to revive their economies.

Despite these efforts, the Great Depression persisted for a decade, and it wasn't until the outbreak of World War II that the global economy began to recover. The war increased government spending, stimulated economic activity, and created jobs.

Lasting impact on the global economy and society. It led to significant changes in economic policy and government intervention in the economy, and it also led to the rise of extremist political movements, such as fascism and communism. The lessons learned from the Great Depression continue to shape economic policy and inform our understanding of economic recessions even today.

Overall, From 1929 through 1939, there was a severe economic downturn known as the Great Depression. Its defining characteristics were high unemployment, low industrial output, and a precipitous decrease in global trade. Governments worldwide tried to combat the depression through various policies and programs, but it wasn't until the outbreak of World War II that the worldwide economy began to recover. Profound and lasting impact on the global economy and society, and its lessons continue to shape economic policy today.

The Great Depression of 1929 affected many countries worldwide, including the United States, Canada, Germany, France, the United Kingdom, Australia, New Zealand, and Japan. Other countries such as Argentina, Brazil, and Chile were also affected. Additionally, many countries in Europe, as well as those in Latin America, Africa, and Asia, were negatively impacted by the economic downturn.

2

Impact on India

The Great Depression of 1929 was a global economic downturn that significantly impacted the Indian economy and the lives of the Indian people. The Indian economy depended heavily on exports, particularly agricultural goods such as cotton, jute, and tea. Demand for these goods fell precipitously due to the drop in global trade during the depression. This resulted in a decrease in prices, which severely impacted the livelihoods of farmers and rural communities.

Farmers and Rural Communities: Farmers and rural communities were among the hardest hit by the economic downturn. The fall in prices for agricultural goods led to a fall in farm incomes, which led to a fall in purchasing power and a decline in economic activity. Many farmers were compelled to sell their land, which led to the impoverishment of many rural households. The lack of government support further exacerbated the suffering of the farmers and rural communities.

Unemployment and Poverty: The fall in demand for goods also affected other sectors of the Indian economy, such as textiles and handicrafts, which were important sources of employment in India at the time. Many textile mills and handicraft units had to close down, leading to high levels of unemployment and poverty.

The lack of government support led to an increase in poverty and social unrest.

Food Insecurity: The fall in agricultural incomes led to a decline in food production, resulting in food shortages and higher food prices. Many people, particularly in rural areas, could not afford to buy enough food to meet their basic needs. This led to increased poverty and malnutrition, which further exacerbated the suffering of the Indian people during the Great Depression.

Limited Government Support: The Indian government's response to the crisis was limited, as it had limited resources and faced financial constraints. It did not implement significant policy measures to stimulate the economy or relieve the affected population. Instead, it relied on traditional measures such as reducing expenditure, increasing taxes, and borrowing from the Reserve Bank of India. This lack of government support further exacerbated the suffering of the Indian people during the Great Depression.

The Great Depression of 1929 had a significant and lasting impact on the Indian economy and the lives of the Indian people. The economic downturn led to high levels of unemployment and poverty, and the lack of government support further exacerbated the suffering of the Indian people. It was not until the Second World War that the Indian economy began to recover.

During the Great Depression of 1929, Indian people's diets were affected by the economic downturn, resulting in food shortages and high food prices. Many struggled to afford enough food to meet their basic needs and were forced to rely on the government to provide food assistance or local charities.

In rural areas, many people's diets were based on staples such as rice, wheat, and millet, which were relatively affordable. However, the fall in agricultural incomes led to a decline in food production, resulting in food shortages and higher food prices. Many people could not afford enough food to meet their basic needs, and many were forced to rely on the government to provide food assistance or local charities for support.

In urban areas, people often had to rely on government-provided food assistance or local charities for support. This usually consisted of basic staples such as flour, sugar, and canned goods. Many urban dwellers also relied on cheap and readily available street food.

Additionally, Indian people used traditional methods to preserve food, such as pickling, drying, and fermentation, to consume food for extended periods. They also used wild fruits and vegetables and foraged for fantastic food to supplement their diets.

Overall, Indian people's diets during the Great Depression were often limited and lacked the variety and nutritional value of more prosperous times. Many people were forced to survive on cheaper, less nutritious food.

3

Lessons Learned

One of the most important economic events of the 20th century was the Great Depression, The depression had a profound impact on the global economy and society, and it also left many valuable lessons for monetary policy and future economic crises.

One critical lesson from the Great Depression is the importance of government intervention in the economy. Before the depression, the prevailing economic philosophy was laissez-faire, which emphasized minimal government interference in the economy. However, the depression demonstrated the limitations of this approach, and it led to a shift toward a more active role for the government in stimulating economic growth and addressing financial problems.

Another important lesson from the Great Depression is the need for economic stimulus during a recession. The government's failure to take action to stimulate the economy during the early years of the depression contributed to the severity and length of the downturn. In contrast, the policies and programs implemented during the New Deal in the United States, such as the Civilian Conservation Corps and the Works Progress Administration, helped to create jobs and stimulate economic activity.

The Great Depression also highlighted the importance of international economic cooperation. The depression was not limited to a single country, and the economic downturn was exacerbated by the lack of collaboration and coordination among nations. The depression led to a decline in international trade and a rise in protectionism, which further deepened the economic downturn. The lessons of the Great Depression led to the creation of institutions such as the International Monetary Fund and the World Bank, which were established to promote international economic cooperation and stability.

The Great Depression also emphasized the need for a sound financial system. The Federal Deposit Protection Corporation (FDIC) was established to offer insurance for bank deposits and assist in stabilizing the banking system related to the United States banking industry's collapse, which also contributed to the severity of the depression.

Finally, the Great Depression taught us the importance of social safety net. The economic hardship experienced by so many during the depression led to a greater awareness of the need for government programs to assist those in need, such as unemployment insurance, social security, and public service.

Overall, The Great Depression from 1929 to 1939; left many valuable lessons for monetary policy and future financial crises. The depression showed the importance of government intervention in the economy, the need for economic stimulus during a recession, the importance of international economic cooperation, a sound financial system, and the importance of social safety net. These lessons continue to shape monetary policy and inform our understanding of economic recessions even today.

Chapter Ten

Hyperinflation

1

Facts of Hyperinflation

Hyper**inflation** is a term used to describe a condition in which the prices of goods and services increase rapidly and out of control. It is characterized by a sustained increase in the general level of goods and services prices, typically over months or years. Hyper**inflation** occurs when there is a significant increase in the money supply and a corresponding decline in the value of money. This can lead to rising prices and decreasing purchasing power, which can have severe economic and social consequences.

One of the most well-known examples of hyper**inflation** occurred in Germany in the early 1920s. After World War I, the German government printed large amounts of money to pay for the war and cover its sizable national debt. As a result, the money supply significantly increased, and the value of the German mark also decreased. Prices began to rise rapidly; by 1923, they were growing at over 10% per day. By November 1923, the **inflation** rate had reached an astronomical level of 29,500% per month. The German economy was severely damaged by **hyperinflation**, and it took many years for the country to recover.

Another example of **hyperinflation** occurred in Yugoslavia in the early 1990s. After the separation from the Soviet Union, Yugoslavia faced a severe economic crisis, with high levels of unemployment and **inflation**. The government responded by printing large amounts of money to cover its budget deficit. As a result, the money supply significantly increased, and the value of the Yugoslav dinar also decreased. Prices began to rise rapidly; by 1993, they were growing at over 50% per month. By January 1994, the **inflation** rate had reached an astronomical level of 313 million percent per month. The Yugoslav economy was severely damaged by **hyperinflation**, and it took many years for the country to recover.

Hyper**inflation** can have severe economic and social consequences. It can lead to a decline in production and a fall in the standard of living. It can also lead to a decrease in the value of savings and investments, making it more difficult for people to plan for the future.

Hyperinflation can also lead to a decline in the value of money, making it more difficult for people to purchase goods and services and decreasing economic activity.

Overall, **hyperinflation** is a severe economic condition characterized by a sustained increase in the general price level of goods and services, typically for months or years. It is caused by a significant increase in the money supply and a corresponding decline in the value of money. The examples of Germany in the 1920s and Yugoslavia in the 1990s illustrate the severe economic and social consequences that can result from **hyperinflation**.

2

Germany

Germany experienced hyper**inflation** in the early 1920s. Had a severe impact on the German people and the economy. After World War I, the German government faced a large national debt and a struggling economy. The government began printing large amounts of money to pay for the war and cover its debt. As a result, the money supply significantly increased, and the value of the German mark also decreased. Prices began to rise rapidly; by 1923, they were growing at over 10% per day.

The effects of hyper**inflation** were devastating for the German people. The rapid price increase made it challenging for people to afford necessities like food and housing. The value of savings and investments was also rapidly declining, making it difficult for people to plan for the future. The decline in purchasing power also led to a decrease in economic activity, resulting in high levels of unemployment and poverty.

The German people also had to deal with a lack of trust in the German mark, which further impacted the economy. People began hoarding goods, which became scarce, increasing prices. Businesses and factories also struggled as they could not keep up with the constant price increase, which led to more unemployment.

The German government's response to the crisis was limited, and the German people had to rely on local charities or traditional methods to survive. The lack of government action further exacerbated the suffering of the German people.

The rapid increase in prices and decline in purchasing power led to a lack of trust in the German mark, and people began to look for alternative forms of currency to use for transactions.

One of the ways that people coped with hyper**inflation** was by using barter trade. People would trade goods and services directly without using the German mark. For example, a farmer might sell a bag of potatoes for shoes. This was especially common in rural areas where the local economy was less impacted by **hyperinflation**.

Another way that people coped with **hyperinflation** was by using foreign currency or other forms of money that were more stable. For example, some people used US dollars, Swiss francs, or gold coins as currency. These alternative forms of money were more stable and had more purchasing power than the German mark.

It's also worth noting that people tried to get rid of their money as fast as possible, before it lost its value, by buying anything they could afford, even if they didn't need it. This led to shortages of goods in the market, as people believed everything they could get their hands on, leading to even higher prices.

Overall, the hyper**inflation** that occurred in Germany in the early 1920s severely impacted the German people and the economy. The rapid increase in prices, decline in purchasing power, high levels of unemployment, and poverty were the direct result of hyper**inflation**. The lack of government action further exacerbated the suffering of the German people. The use of fiat currency, which is not backed by any tangible assets, and the government's decision to print large amounts of money to cover its debt played a significant role in causing hyper**inflation**. As a result, people lost faith in their currency. They turned to other means of exchange, such as bartering goods and services and using foreign currency or other forms of money, such as gold and silver, which were considered more stable to cope with hyperinflation and the lack of trust in the German mark.

3

Sri Lanka

Sri Lanka, a beautiful island country in South Asia, has a rich history and culture. However, in recent years, the government has faced a significant economic challenge in the form of hyper**inflation**. How has it affected Sri Lanka, and what measures have been taken to address this issue?

Sri Lanka has experienced hyper**inflation**, with the most recent episode occurring in the late 1970s and early 1980s. During this period, the annual **inflation** rate reached as high as 200%, and the country's economy was in a crisis.

Hyper**inflation** in Sri Lanka began in the late 2000s due to high government spending, a large budget deficit, and a balance of payments crisis. 2011 saw the peak of the **inflation** rate, which was over 20%.

In 2022 April **inflation** is at 17.5 percent, with prices of food items such as a kilogram of rice soaring to 500 Sri Lankan rupees when it typically costs around 80 rupees. During shortages, one 400g packet of milk powder is reported to cost over 250 rupees when it usually costs approximately 60 rupees. The country's economy was once again in a state of turmoil.

On April 1, President Gotabaya Rajapaksa declared a state of emergency. In less than a week, he withdrew it following massive protests by angry citizens over the government's handling of the crisis.

The government of Sri Lanka has implemented many measures, including tightening monetary policy, reducing government spending, and implementing structural reforms to improve the country's balance of payments.

Despite progress in addressing hyper**inflation**, Sri Lanka still faces economic challenges. The country's debt-to-GDP ratio is high, and the government has had to implement austerity measures to address the budget deficit. Additionally, the country's economy has been impacted by the COVID-19 pandemic, leading to decreased economic activity and increased unemployment.

Sri Lanka is a high cost of importing goods. Sri Lanka heavily depends on imports for its energy and food needs, and its trade balance has been in deficit for many years. Due to the significant level of foreign debt that has resulted, the country's balance of payments is under strain.

In addition to monetary and fiscal policies, the government of Sri Lanka has also implemented several structural reforms to address the problem of hyper**inflation**. These include measures to increase the public sector's efficiency and promote private sector development. The government has also liberalized the economy, including reducing trade barriers and encouraging foreign investment.

Despite the steps taken to combat hyper**inflation**, the nation faces some economic difficulties. The unemployment rate in Sri Lanka remains high, and the country's public debt is among the highest in the world. The government will need to continue implementing policies to address these challenges and maintain its efforts to combat hyper**inflation**.

Gold price is at an all-time high, 22 Carat 8 Grams (1 Pawn). Gold Price Today in Sri Lanka is Rs. 181,100 as of January 27, 2023. You can buy 22 Carat 1 Gram of Gold for Rs. 22,640. 24 Carat 8 Grams Gold rate is Rs. 197,500.

4

Time for Gold & Silver

During hyperinflation, gold and silver were relatively stable stores of value compared to fiat currencies. Hyper**inflation** is a severe economic condition characterized by a sustained increase in the general price level of goods and services, typically over months or years. It is caused by a significant increase in the money supply and a corresponding decline in the value of money. As the local currency loses value rapidly, gold and silver remain relatively stable.

In particular, gold has a long history of serving as both a store of value and an **inflation** hedge. It has been considered a store of wealth for centuries and is not directly tied to the local currency or economy. As a result, gold can retain its value during hyper**inflation**, as it is not subject to the same forces that drive **inflation** in the local currency.

Silver, on the other hand, is also considered an **inflation** hedge and a store of value. Silver has traditionally been used as a currency and has been considered a store of wealth for centuries. Silver is also relatively scarce and is used in many industrial applications. The industrial demand for silver can support its value even during hyper**inflation**.

During hyper**inflation**, people tend to lose trust in their local currency and may look for alternative forms of preserving their wealth. Some people may turn to gold and silver to protect their savings from the effects of hyper**inflation**. As the local currency loses value, gold and silver's relative value increases, making them more attractive options as stores of wealth.

During periods of extreme **inflation**, investing in gold and silver can help protect wealth and preserve purchasing power. This can be done by buying physical gold and silver, such as bullion, coins, or jewelry, or by investing in gold and silver-related financial products such as exchange-traded funds (ETFs) or mining stocks.

However, it is essential to note that gold and silver are not entirely immune to market fluctuations. Their prices can also be affected by global economic conditions and other factors. Therefore, before making any investment decisions, it is crucial to do your research and speak with a financial counselor. Additionally, it's also important to be aware of the potential risks and limitations associated with holding physical gold and silver, such as storage and insurance costs.

Overall, during hyperinflation, gold and silver were relatively stable stores of value compared to fiat currencies. As the local currency loses value rapidly, gold and silver remain relatively stable. Having gold and silver during times of **hyperinflation** can be a way to protect wealth and maintain purchasing power. Still, it's essential to consider the potential risks and limitations before making investment decisions.

Chapter Eleven

Rupee Digitalization

1

Digital Currency

Digital currency, also known as digital money or electronic money, is a currency that exists only in digital form and is not backed by a physical commodity. It is typically created, managed, and exchanged using computer networks and software. Examples of digital currencies include Bitcoin, Ethereum, and Litecoin.

Bitcoin, the first decentralized digital money, was released in January 2009 by an individual or group using the pseudonym "Satoshi Nakamoto." The source code of the Bitcoin software was published as an open-source project, and the first bitcoins were issued through a process called "mining." Bitcoin is decentralized, not controlled by any government or institution, and transactions are recorded on a people/public ledger called the blockchain.

Since then, many other digital currencies have been introduced, such as Ethereum, Litecoin, and Ripple. These digital currencies, also known as "altcoins" (short for "alternative coins"), are similar to Bitcoin in that they are decentralized and use blockchain technology. Still, they have their own unique features and use cases.

The introduction of digital currencies has significantly impacted the financial industry and led to the creation of a new asset class known as "cryptocurrency." It has also introduced new financial technologies such as decentralized finance (Defi) and smart contracts.

Digital currency is still considered a relatively new technology, and its future development and acceptance are uncertain. Some countries have embraced and started regulating it, while others have outright banned it. And its value is also highly volatile, making it a high-risk investment.

2

India Digital Rupee

A digital version of the Indian rupee may one day be issued, according to the Reserve Bank of India (RBI). It has been known as a "rupee digital currency" or "digital rupee" for quite some time now. The idea is to promote a cashless society and make transactions more convenient and secure for citizens.

The RBI (Reserve Bank of India) established an interdepartmental panel in 2019 to investigate the "Possibility and desire" of releasing a digital version of the rupee. The committee was tasked with researching the technical, legal, and regulatory requirements and other aspects of a digital rupee. Using blockchain technology to assure security and transparency, the government declared in 2020 that it was developing a "conceptual framework" for a digital rupee.

The government's push toward a digital economy is also reflected in its ambitious plans for the launch of a new digital identification system called "Aadhaar," which aims to provide a unique identity to every resident of India. This will make it easier for citizens to open bank accounts, access government services, and complete transactions online. The government also launched Bharat Interface for Money (BHIM) to promote digital transactions, a mobile app that allows users to make payments through UPI. It's also a step forward to get more people comfortable with digital transactions.

Despite these efforts, a significant portion of the population in India still relies on cash transactions and is only partially comfortable with digital payments. This is where the introduction of the digital rupee currency comes in. It will be more accessible to people, as it will be a digital rupee that can be easily stored on a mobile phone or a computer. This will make it more convenient for people to complete transactions, especially in rural areas where access to banks and ATMs can be limited.

It's important to note that the government still needs to provide a precise launch date for the digital rupee, which is still in the research stage. The government and RBI are, nevertheless, making all necessary preparations to guarantee the safety, openness, and accessibility of the digital rupee. When it is introduced, the digital rupee would completely transform the Indian economy by speeding up and simplifying user transactions, fostering financial inclusion, and eliminating reliance on cash.

3

Digital Currency Theft

One of the main concerns with digital currencies is that they are stored in digital wallets, which can be hacked if the user's device or server is not secured correctly. For example, in January 2018, a South Korean cryptocurrency exchange called Coincheck was hacked and lost around $530 million worth of digital currency. The hack occurred because the conversation needed proper security measures to protect the digital currency stored on its servers.

Hackers can also steal digital currency by gaining access to a user's private key, which is used to authorize transactions. Each user has a private key, a lengthy string of numbers and characters to access the digital currency in their digital wallet. If a hacker can obtain a user's private key, they can use it to steal the user's digital money.

Additionally, some digital currencies are stored on decentralized networks, such as blockchain, where a hacker can take control of many nodes and create an alternate version of the blockchain. This is called a "51% attack" or double-spend attack. This could allow the hacker to spend the same digital currency multiple times, effectively counterfeiting it. For example, in May 2019, a 51% attack occurred on the Ethereum Classic (ETC) blockchain, resulting in the theft of around $1.1 million worth of ETC.

However, it's worth noting that many digital currencies have implemented advanced security measures to protect against hacking and cybercrime. For example, some digital currencies use multi-signature technology, which requires multiple private keys to authorize a transaction.

Hackers will find it more challenging to steal virtual money as a result. Additionally, many digital currencies use advanced encryption techniques to protect users' private keys. Some also use cold storage, which is a way of storing digital currency offline to prevent hacking.

Users need to protect their digital money by using strong and unique passwords, keeping their devices and software updated, and avoiding suspicious links or attachments in emails or messages. And it's also essential to store digital money in a well-known and reputable wallet rather than to store a large amount of money in a single wallet.

Sure, here are a few more examples of digital currency-related hacks:

- In January 2021, the Twitter accounts of several high-profile individuals and companies were hacked and used to promote a scam in which users were asked to send Bitcoin to a specific address in exchange for double the amount sent. This scam resulted in the theft of around $120,000 worth of Bitcoin.
- In March 2021, the popular digital currency exchange Binance was hacked, resulting in the theft of around $60 million worth of various digital currencies. Binance later announced that it would cover the losses suffered by its users from its own funds. Still, it highlights the

importance of using a reputable exchange with robust security measures.

- In December 2021, a hacker exploited a vulnerability in the smart contract of the decentralized finance (Defi) platform, known as Harvest Finance, and stole more than $24 million in various digital currencies. This incident shows that even decentralized platforms, generally considered more secure, can be vulnerable to attacks.

These examples demonstrate that digital currency is not immune to hacking and other cybercrime and that users need to take steps to protect their digital money. It's important to keep software updated, use strong and unique passwords, and store digital currency in reputable wallets and exchanges with robust security measures.

Overall, while the digital currency has many advantages, it's not immune to vulnerabilities. Users must protect their digital money and be cautious of the wallet or exchange they are using. It's also important to note that the technology behind digital currency is still evolving, and new security measures and solutions are being developed all the time to address these vulnerabilities.

4

No Internet, No Digital Currency

When there is no internet, digital currency is severely limited. Transactions would not be able to be processed, and it would be difficult for users to access their digital wallets. Additionally, without internet connectivity, it would not be easy to verify transactions on the blockchain, which is the technology that underlies most digital currencies. This would make it difficult for digital currencies to function as intended and potentially lead to a loss of confidence in the digital currency. You may have experienced this in your daily life pattern.

Let's see some examples of instances where internet connectivity has been shut down or restricted in India:

1. In 2019, the Indian government ordered internet service providers to shut down internet connectivity in Jammu and Kashmir after the revocation of the region's autonomy.

2. In 2020, the Indian government ordered internet service providers to shut down internet connectivity in several districts of the state of Assam following widespread protests against the Citizenship Amendment Act.

3. In 2020, the Indian government ordered internet service providers to shut down internet connectivity in several

districts of the state of West Bengal following widespread protests against the Citizenship Amendment Act.

4. In 2020, The Indian government ordered internet service providers to shut down internet connectivity in several districts of the state of Uttar Pradesh following widespread protests against the Citizenship Amendment Act.

5. In 2020, The Indian government ordered internet service providers to shut down internet connectivity in several districts of the state of Delhi following widespread protests against the Citizenship Amendment Act.

6. In 2020, The Indian government ordered internet service providers to shut down internet connectivity in several districts of the state of Rajasthan following widespread protests against the Citizenship Amendment Act.

7. In 2020, The Indian government ordered internet service providers to shut down internet connectivity in several districts of the state of Gujarat following widespread protests against the Citizenship Amendment Act.

8. In 2020, The Indian government ordered internet service providers to shut down internet connectivity in several districts of the state of Haryana following widespread protests against the Citizenship Amendment Act.

9. In 2020, The Indian government ordered internet service providers to shut down internet connectivity in several districts of the state of Maharashtra following widespread protests against the Citizenship Amendment Act.

There have been a few instances where countries have temporarily or permanently shut down internet connectivity, often suppressing dissent or controlling the flow of information. Some examples include:

1. China has temporarily shut down internet connectivity in certain regions, such as Xinjiang and Tibet, to control the flow of information and suppress dissent.
2. During the Arab Spring in 2011, several countries in North Africa and the ME (Middle East), including Egypt, Libya, and Syria, shut down internet connectivity to control information flow and suppress dissent.
3. In 2020, the government of Iran cut off internet access during the widespread protests over the death of a famous wrestler.
4. In 2021, Myanmar's military junta shut down the internet and mobile networks nationwide to quell the pro-democracy protests against the coup d'etat.
5. In 2021, Ethiopia's government shut down internet connectivity in the Tigray region following military operations, making it difficult for residents to communicate and access information.
6. In 2021, The Chad government shut down the internet for a week in the lead-up to the presidential elections to prevent the spreading fake news and misinformation.
7. In 2021, The Venezuelan government shut down internet connectivity in several regions to quell anti-government protests.
8. In 2021, The Belarus government shut down internet connectivity in several regions to quell anti-government protests.
9. In 2021, The Uganda government shut down internet connectivity during the general elections to prevent the spreading of fake news and misinformation.

The above examples are incomplete, and in some cases, the internet connection was resumed after some period. Some states in India have also implemented internet censorship and control over certain websites and online content, even when internet connectivity is not entirely shut down.

5

Gold as Digital Currency

More and more people are now considering using gold as virtual money. This is due to several factors, including how well-liked digital currencies are becoming, how much demand there is for a reliable store of value, and how simple it is to purchase and sell gold online.

The advantage of using gold as a digital currency is that it is a stable store of value. Unlike fiat currencies, which can depreciate over time due to **inflation**, the value of gold tends to remain relatively stable. This makes it an attractive option for individuals and organizations looking to protect their wealth from the effects of **inflation**.

Another benefit of using gold as a digital currency is that it is a decentralized form of money. Unlike traditional fiat currencies controlled by governments and central banks, gold is not subject to the same level of manipulation and control. This makes it a more secure and reliable form of currency for transactions.

There are many ways to use gold as a digital currency. One popular option is to use a digital gold token, such as a stablecoin, which is pegged to the value of gold. These tokens can be easily bought and sold on digital currency exchanges. They can be used for transactions similarly to traditional fiat currencies.

Some Advantages:

- **Stability:** Gold has been a store of value for centuries, and its value tends to remain relatively stable. This makes it an attractive option for individuals and organizations looking to protect their wealth from the effects of **inflation**.

- **Decentralization:** Gold is not subject to the same level of manipulation and control as traditional fiat currencies controlled by governments and central banks. This makes it a more secure and reliable form of money for transactions.

- **Liquidity:** With the introduction of digital gold tokens and internet marketplaces, anyone may purchase and trade gold. Turning gold into cash or other forms of money is more straightforward than ever.

- **Portability:** Digital gold can be easily stored and transferred in a digital format, making it more convenient for individuals and organizations to hold and trade gold.

- **Accessibility:** Gold can be bought and sold online, which makes it accessible to a broader range of individuals and organizations, regardless of their location.

- **Transparency:** Digital gold platforms provide real-time information on the price of gold, making it easier for individuals and organizations to track the value of their investments.

- **Flexibility:** Digital gold tokens and contracts provide individuals and organizations with greater flexibility in terms of how they hold and trade gold, allowing them to use various trading strategies.

- **Diversification:** An investment portfolio can benefit from an additional layer of diversity by holding gold as a digital currency.
- **Convenience:** Platforms and tokens for digital gold make it simple for people to purchase and sell gold anywhere in the world.

Chapter Twelve

Scams

1

Bank's and it's Scam's

Banking scams are a sad reality in today's world. They can happen to anyone at any time and result in significant financial losses. I aim to educate you on the different banking scams and how they can cheat you. By being aware of these con games. You may take precautions to safeguard yourself and your hard-earned money.

One of the most common banking scams is the phishing scam. When a fraudster sends a text or mail that seems to be coming from a reliable bank or financial institution, the message will typically ask you to click on a link, taking you to a fake website that looks like the real thing. Once on the fake website, you may be asked to enter personal information, such as your social security number, credit card number, or login credentials. This information can lead to stealing your identity or gaining access to your bank account.

Another type of banking scam is the advance fee scam. This is when a scammer contacts you and tells you that you have won a large sum of money, but to claim the prize, you must first pay a fee. The scammer may ask for a small amount of money upfront but will then keep asking for more and more. Eventually, you will realize that you have been scammed and will never receive the prize money.

A third type of banking scam is the investment scam. This is when a scammer convinces you to invest in a company or investment opportunity that does not exist. The scammer will often use high-pressure tactics to persuade you to support and will promise unrealistic returns on your investment. Once you have invested your money, the scammer will disappear, leaving you with no way to get your money back.

A fourth type of banking scam is the credit card scam. This is when a scammer gets your credit card information and makes unauthorized purchases. It is essential to keep your credit card information secure and monitor your credit card statement regularly to ensure there are no unauthorized charges.

It's essential to be vigilant and to take steps to safeguard your personal and financial information. Always be suspicious of unsolicited phone calls, emails, or text messages, and never click on links or enter personal information into a website you are unfamiliar with. Monitor your bank account and credit card statements regularly to ensure no unauthorized transactions. When you suspect you have been a victim of a banking scam, immediately contact your bank or financial institution and report the incident to the authorities.

Overall, banking scams are a reality that we must all be aware of. They can happen to anyone at any time and result in significant financial losses. By being aware of these scams and taking steps to protect yourself, you can help to ensure that your money stays safe and secure.

India Scam List:

These are just some of the notable bank scams that have occurred in India.. As the Indian banking sector grows, more and more sophisticated scams are appearing. It's important to note that the Indian government and financial regulators have strengthened regulations and oversight to prevent such fraud in the future. The bank scams are not unique to India. They happen in many countries.

1. The Harshad Mehta Scandal (1992): This scam, also known as the "Big Bull" scam, involved securities fraud and manipulation by stockbroker Harshad Mehta. The scam led to a loss of over $1 billion and resulted in the stock market's collapse.
2. The Ketan Parekh Scandal (2001): This scam involved securities fraud and manipulation by stockbroker Ketan

Parekh. The scam led to a loss of over $1 billion and resulted in the collapse of several financial institutions.

3. The Satyam Scandal (2009): This scam, also known as the "India's Enron" scandal, involved fraud and accounting irregularities at Satyam Computer Services, a prominent Indian IT company. The scandal led to a loss of over $2 billion and resulted in the company's collapse.

4. The PNB Scam (2018): This scam, also known as the Nirav Modi scam, involved fraudulent letters of undertaking issued by employees of the Punjab National Bank (PNB), one of India's largest public sector banks. The fraud led to a loss of over $2 billion and resulted in the resignation of the bank's CEO.

5. The HDFC Bank Scam (2020): This scam, also known as the "Housing Development Finance Corporation" scam, involved a group of individuals who allegedly used insider information to fraudulently obtain large loans from the bank. The fraud led to a loss of over $1.8 billion and resulted in the arrest of several bank officials.

6. The Syndicate Bank Scam (1991): This scam involved the fraudulent withdrawal of crores of rupees from various branches of the Syndicate Bank by a group of individuals. This was one of the first central bank scams in India.

7. The IDBI Bank Scam (2019): This scam involved a group of individuals who allegedly fraudulently obtained large loans from IDBI Bank by providing false information. The fraud resulted in a loss of over $1 billion and the arrest of several bank officials.

8. The PMC Bank Scam (2019): This scam involved a group of individuals who allegedly fraudulently obtained large

loans from the Punjab and Maharashtra Cooperative Bank (PMC Bank) by providing false information. The fraud resulted in a loss of over $2 billion and the arrest of several bank officials.

9. The ICICI Bank Scam (2019): This scam involved a group of individuals who allegedly fraudulently obtained large loans from ICICI Bank by providing false information. The fraud resulted in a loss of over $1 billion and the arrest of several bank officials.

10. The Andhra Bank Scam (2015): This scam, also known as the "Vijay Mallya Scam," involved a group of individuals who allegedly fraudulently obtained large loans from Andhra Bank by providing false information. The scam resulted in a loss of over $1 billion and resulted in the arrest of several bank officials.

11. The Axis Bank Scam (2016): This scam involved a group of individuals who allegedly fraudulently obtained large loans from Axis Bank by providing false information. The fraud resulted in a loss of over $1 billion and the arrest of several bank officials.

12. The Allahabad Bank Scam (2017): This scam involved a group of individuals who allegedly fraudulently obtained large loans from Allahabad Bank by providing false information. The fraud resulted in a loss of over $1 billion and the arrest of several bank officials.

13. The Canara Bank Scam (2018): This scam involved a group of individuals who allegedly fraudulently obtained large loans from Canara Bank by providing false information. The fraud resulted in a loss of over $1 billion and the arrest of several bank officials.

14. The SBI Scam (2018): This scam involved a group of individuals who allegedly fraudulently obtained large loans from the State Bank of India (SBI) by providing false information. The fraud resulted in a loss of over $1 billion and the arrest of several bank officials.

15. The UBI Scam (2019): This scam involved a group of individuals who allegedly fraudulently obtained large loans from the Union Bank of India (UBI) by providing false information. The fraud resulted in a loss of over $1 billion and the arrest of several bank officials.

16. The BoB-SBM Scam (2019): This scam involved a group of individuals who allegedly fraudulently obtained large loans from the Bank of Baroda (BoB) and the State Bank of Mauritius (SBM) by providing false information. The scam resulted in a loss of over $1 billion and resulted in the arrest of several bank officials.

17. The Karur Vysya Bank Scam (2021): This scam involved a group of individuals who allegedly fraudulently obtained large loans from the Karur Vysya Bank by providing false information. The fraud resulted in a loss of over $100 million and the arrest of several bank officials.

18. The Dena Bank Scam (2021): This scam involved a group of individuals who allegedly fraudulently obtained large loans from Dena Bank by providing false information. The fraud resulted in a loss of over $200 million and the arrest of several bank officials.

19. The UCO Bank Scam (2022): This scam involved a group of individuals who allegedly fraudulently obtained large loans from the UCO Bank by providing false information. The fraud resulted in a loss of over $50 million and the arrest of several bank officials.

20. The Indian Overseas Bank Scam (2022): This scam involved a group of individuals who allegedly fraudulently obtained large loans from the Indian Overseas Bank by providing false information. The fraud resulted in a loss of over $100 million and the arrest of several bank officials.

Around The World Bank Scam List:

There have been many bank scams worldwide, so it would not be easy to list them here. It will become a scam dictionary. However, here are some notable bank scams that have occurred in various countries:

1. The Savings and Loan Crisis (the 1980s-1990s) in the United States: This scam involved a group of individuals' fraudulent withdrawal of billions of dollars from savings and loan associations.

2. The BCCI Scandal (1991) in the United Kingdom and other countries: This scam involved fraud and money laundering by the Bank of Credit and Commerce International (BCCI).

3. The Barings Bank Scandal (1995) in the United Kingdom: This scam involved securities fraud and unauthorized trading by Nick Leeson, a trader at Barings Bank.

4. The Enron Scandal (2001) in the United States: This scam involved fraud and accounting irregularities at Enron, a major energy company.

5. The Madoff Scandal (2008) in the United States: This scam involved a Ponzi scheme by Bernard Madoff, a financial adviser.

6. The Nordea Scandal (2013) in Denmark: This scam involved money laundering and other financial crimes by Nordea Bank.

7. The Wells Fargo Scandal (2016) in the United States: This scam involved opening unauthorized accounts by Wells Fargo employees.

8. The Commonwealth Bank Scandal (2017) in Australia: This scam involved money laundering and other financial crimes by the Commonwealth Bank of Australia.

9. The Danske Bank Scandal (2018) in Denmark: This scam involved money laundering and other financial crimes by Danske Bank.

10. The UBS Scandal (2010) in Switzerland: This scam involved the manipulation of the London Interbank Offered Rate (LIBOR) by UBS employees.

11. The Standard Chartered Scandal (2012) in the United Kingdom: This scam involved money laundering and other financial crimes by Standard Chartered Bank.

12. The Deutsche Bank Scandal (2016) in Germany: This scam involved foreign exchange market manipulation by Deutsche Bank employees.

13. The Societe Generale Scandal (2016) in France: This scam involved the manipulation of the foreign exchange market by Societe Generale employees.

14. The Rabobank Scandal (2013) in the Netherlands: This scam involved the manipulation of the London Interbank Offered Rate (LIBOR) by Rabobank employees.

15. The Credit Suisse Scandal (2014) in Switzerland: This scam involved manipulation of the foreign exchange market by Credit Suisse employees.

16. The JP Morgan Scandal (2013) in the United States: This scam involved the manipulation of the foreign exchange market by JP Morgan employees.

17. The BNP Paribas Scandal (2014) in France: This scam involved money laundering and other financial crimes by BNP Paribas.

18. The Royal Bank of Scotland Scandal (2013) in the United Kingdom: This scam involved foreign exchange market manipulation by Royal Bank of Scotland employees.

19. The Mizuho Scandal (2013) in Japan: This scam involved money laundering and other financial crimes by Mizuho Bank.

20. The Westpac Scandal (2020) in Australia: This scam involved money laundering and other financial crimes by Westpac Bank.

Again, this is not an exhaustive list and many more bank scams have occurred worldwide over the years, but I hope this gives you an idea of some notable examples.

Systematic Investment Plan (SIP) and Its Scams

Systematic Investment Plan (SIP) is India's most recommended investment option that allows individuals to invest a fixed amount at regular intervals, usually monthly, into mutual funds. The convenience and flexibility of SIPs make them an ideal choice for people who want to invest in mutual funds but may not have a big lump sum of money to invest at once.

One of the most significant advantages of SIPs is that they enable investors to take advantage of the power of compounding. Compounding refers to the process where the returns earned on an investment are reinvested to generate even more returns. Over time, this may lead to significant growth in the value of the investment. By investing small amounts of money at regular intervals, SIPs can help investors achieve their financial goals in the long term.

The impact of market volatility is lessened, which is another advantage of SIPs. When investing in a lump sum, the value of the investment is determined by the market conditions. With SIPs, investors can purchase units at different prices, which helps reduce the impact of market fluctuations.

SIPs are also a great way to inculcate the habit of saving and investing for the future. Investing a small amount at regular intervals makes it easy to set aside money for the future without feeling the pinch in the present. Additionally, SIPs are flexible and can be stopped, paused, or resumed at one's convenience.

SIPs are available for most mutual funds, including equity, debt, and balanced funds. Equity funds invest primarily in stocks and are suitable for investors with a high-risk tolerance and a long-term investment horizon. On the other hand, debt funds invest mainly in fixed-income securities such as bonds and are suitable for investors with lower risk tolerance and a shorter-term investment horizon. Funds balanced invest in stocks and bonds and are ideal for investors with moderate risk tolerance.

To start a SIP, one needs to approach a mutual fund company and fill out an application form. The investor will then need to provide their personal and financial details and choose the mutual fund they wish to invest in. Investors will also need to decide on the amount they want to invest and the frequency of the investment. Once the application is processed, the investor will be sent a mandate form, which they will need to sign and return to the mutual fund company.

Overall, SIPs are a great investment option for people who want to invest in mutual funds but may not have a large lump sum of money to invest at once. The convenience and flexibility of SIPs make them an ideal choice for people who want to benefit from the power of compounding and reduce the impact of market volatility. SIPs also help to inculcate the habit of saving and investing for the future and are available for most mutual funds. If you're interested in starting a SIP, approach a mutual fund company and fill out an application form. With a SIP, you can work toward achieving your financial goals with ease and convenience.

It is essential to be aware of potential scams when investing in a Systematic Investment Plan (SIP), as they can lead to losing money. Here are a few examples of common SIP scams:

1. **Ponzi Schemes:** A Ponzi scheme Promises investors high returns with minimum to no risk. However, the returns are generated by new investors' funds rather than any legitimate investment activity.

2. **Unauthorized Transactions:** Some fraudsters may use your personal information to make unauthorized transactions or investments on your behalf.

3. **False Promises:** Some scammers may promise unrealistic returns or guarantee that the investment is risk-free, which is impossible in any investment.

4. **Impersonation:** Scammers may impersonate legitimate investment companies or representatives to gain your trust and trick you into investing.

5. **Pressure Tactics:** Scammers may use pressure tactics to convince you to invest as quickly as possible before you have a chance to research the investment or consider the risks.

6. **Phishing Scams:** Scammers may use phishing emails or text messages to trick you into providing personal information or transferring funds to a fraudulent account.

7. **Misrepresentation of Funds:** Some scammers may misrepresent the nature of the funds being invested, such as claiming that they are invested in low-risk or high-return assets when they are actually invested in high-risk or low-return investments.

8. **Unregistered Investment Companies:** Some scammers may operate unlisted investment companies and may not be subject to the same regulations and oversight as legitimate investment companies.

9. **Limited Information:** Some scammers may need to provide more accurate information about the investment, such as hiding the risks or exaggerating the potential returns.

10. **Withdrawal Restrictions:** Some scammers may restrict the ability to withdraw funds from the investment, making it difficult or impossible to access your money when needed.

11. **Pressure to Recruit:** Some scammers may pressure you to recruit others to invest in the SIP scam, promising you will receive a commission or bonus.
12. **Inflated Appraisals:** Some scammers may inflate the value of the assets being invested in, making the investment appear more attractive.

It is important to remember that if an investment sounds too good to be true, it probably is. Always be wary of unsolicited offers and do your own research before investing. It's also important to be suspicious if you are pressured to invest quickly or if there needs to be more transparency about the investment. It's better to invest your money in what you can afford to lose and diversify your investment.

3

Mutual Funds and its Scams

Think of a mutual fund as a big basket with lots of different investments, like fruits in a fruit basket. When you buy a share in a mutual fund, it's like getting a little piece of the basket.

A professional manager is responsible for picking what goes into the basket and ensuring it's always full of healthy, tasty investments. So, instead of selecting individual assets, you can relax while the fund manager does the work for you.

As the investments in the basket grow and change in value, so does the value of your share. And when you want to get your money back, you can sell your stake and get a piece of the basket's worth.

Investing in a mutual fund is a convenient and easy way to get a diverse mix of investments without having to do all the research and decision-making yourself.

Let's see some common types of mutual fund scams in India and what investors can do to protect themselves.

Ponzi Schemes: Ponzi schemes are a sort of investment fraud in which profits from legitimate business operations are used to pay returns to existing investors rather than money given by new investors.

Misrepresentation of Returns: Some mutual fund schemes may falsely represent investors' expected returns. This can be done by exaggerating past returns or making unrealistic projections about future returns. Investors should always be wary of schemes that promise high returns with tiny or no risk.

Fake Mutual Funds: In some cases, scammers may create fake mutual funds, using the names of legitimate funds to deceive investors. These fake funds may also falsely represent the returns that investors can expect to earn.

Before making an investment, you must conduct due diligence. Here are a few steps:

- Research the mutual fund you are considering investing in. Look for information about the fund's performance, management team, and expenses.

- Verify the credentials of the mutual fund company and its representatives. Ensure they are registered with the Securities and Exchange Board of India (SEBI).
- Be wary of schemes that promise high returns with little or no risk. Remember that all investments come with some level of risk.
- Stay away from pressure tactics. A legitimate investment opportunity will not require you to make a quick decision and will only pressure you to invest in what you are comfortable with.
- If you suspect a mutual fund scam, report it to the SEBI or local police.

India Mutual Fund Scam List:

Here is a list of some notable instances of mutual fund scams in India:

1. The Sahara Scam (2010-2012): This Scam involved the illegal raising of funds by Sahara India Pariwar through the issuance of optionally fully convertible debentures (OFCDs). The Scam resulted in a loss of over $4 billion for investors.
2. The Franklin Templeton Scam (2021): This Scam involved the illegal freezing of 6 debt funds from Franklin Templeton India's mutual funds, resulting in the loss of thousands of crores to investors.
3. The Ponzi Scam (2018-2019): This Scam involved a Ponzi scheme where a company, PACL India Limited, raised money from the public through illegal means and promised returns to investors but used the money for other purposes. The Scam resulted in a loss of over $8 billion for investors.

4. The Saradha Scam (2013): This Scam involved a Ponzi scheme where the Saradha Group of companies raised money from the public through illegal means and promised returns to investors but used the money for other purposes. The Scam resulted in a loss of over $5 billion for investors.

5. The QNet Scam (2017): This Scam involved a pyramid scheme where QNet, an e-commerce company, raised money from the public by promising returns from investments but used the money for other purposes. The Scam resulted in a loss of over $2 billion for investors.

6. The UTI Scam (2001-2002): This Scam involved the illegal transfer of funds by the Unit Trust of India (UTI) to specific companies, resulting in a loss of over $1 billion for investors.

7. The Reliance Mutual Fund Scam (2008): This Scam involved the mis-selling of Reliance Mutual Fund schemes by Reliance Capital, resulting in a loss of over $500 million for investors.

8. The Sundaram Mutual Fund Scam (2019): This Scam involved the mis-selling of Sundaram Mutual Fund schemes by Sundaram Asset Management Company, resulting in a loss of over $250 million for investors.

9. The Axis Mutual Fund Scam (2021): This Scam involved the mis-selling of Axis Mutual Fund schemes by Axis Asset Management Company, resulting in a loss of over $200 million for investors.

10. The Kotak Mutual Fund Scam (2022): This Scam involved the mis-selling of Kotak Mutual Fund schemes by Kotak Mahindra Asset Management Company, resulting in a loss of over $150 million for investors.

Mutual funds can be a terrific alternative for investors, but it's important to be aware of the chance for fraud. By doing your due diligence, being aware of common types of scams, and not falling for pressure tactics, you can help protect yourself from becoming a victim of mutual fund fraud.

Around The World Mutual Scam List:

These are just examples of mutual fund scams that have occurred worldwide, and the data may not be accurate.

1. Bernard Madoff's Ponzi scheme in the US, in which he stole billions of dollars from investors (2008).
2. The collapse of the Canadian investment firm Nortel Networks resulted in the loss of billions of dollars for investors (2009)
3. The collapse of the Reserve Primary Fund in the US, which was a significant player in the 2008 financial crisis (2008)
4. The Luxembourg-based investment company KBC Asset Management was found to have defrauded investors out of millions of dollars (2003)
5. The collapse of the Pirate Investor Fund in Iceland resulted in significant losses for investors (2009)
6. The collapse of the Petters Group Worldwide in the US, which defrauded investors of billions of dollars (2008)
7. The Stanford Financial Group scam in the US, in which investors lost billions of dollars (2009)
8. The collapse of the Belgian-French Fortis Bank resulted in significant losses for investors (2008)
9. The Madoff Investment Securities LLC scam in the US, in which investors lost billions of dollars (2008)

10. The Allen Stanford Ponzi scheme in the US, in which investors lost billions of dollars (2009)

11. The AIG Financial Products Scandal in the US, in which investors lost billions of dollars (2008)

12. The Colonial Bank Scandal in the US, in which investors lost millions of dollars (2009)

13. The Westpoint Corp Scandal in Australia, in which investors lost millions of dollars (2006)

14. The Tri-West Investment Scandal in Canada, in which investors lost millions of dollars (2005)

15. The Robert Allen Stanford Ponzi scheme in the US, in which investors lost billions of dollars (2009)

16. The AIG Financial Products Scandal in the US, in which investors lost billions of dollars (2008)

17. The Colonial Bank Scandal in the US, in which investors lost millions of dollars (2009)

18. The Westpoint Corp Scandal in Australia, in which investors lost millions of dollars (2006)

4

Stock Market and its Scams

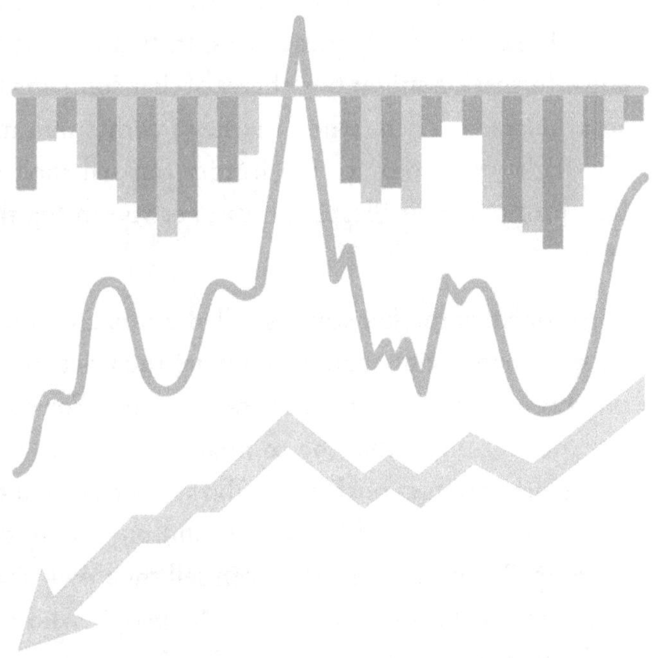

The stock market is like a big marketplace where you can buy and sell parts of companies, called stocks or shares. When you buy a share of a company, you become a tiny part-owner of that company. As the business expands and gains value, the value of your share can also increase.

The stock market operates on a system of supply and demand. If many people want to buy shares in a company, the price of those shares will go up. And, if many people want to sell their shares, the price will go down. This is why the stock market can be a bit like a rollercoaster, with prices constantly increasing.

Now, just like any marketplace, the stock market can also be where scams and shady dealings can happen. One type of scam is called insider trading, which occurs when people with inside information about a company use that information to make money in the stock market. For example, suppose a company is about to release some really great news. In that case, someone with inside information might buy shares of that company before the report is released. Then, when the news comes out and the company's stock price goes up, the insider can sell their shares and make a profit. This is illegal and can get you in big trouble with the law.

Another type of stock market scam is called pump and dump. In this scam, scammers try to artificially inflate the price of a stock by spreading false information about the company. For example, they might spread rumors that the company is about to release a revolutionary new product or that it is about to be bought out. If enough people believe these false rumors and buy the stock, the price will go up. Then, the scammers can sell their own shares at a larger price and make a profit, leaving the people who bought in later with worthless stock.

So, how can you protect yourself from stock market scams? Firstly, always do your research and be cautious of too-good-to-be-true investment opportunities. Secondly, be aware of red flags, such as pressure to invest quickly or promises of guaranteed returns. And finally, if you need clarification on an investment, feel free to seek advice from a financial professional or the authorities.

Overall, the stock market can be a great way to grow your money. Still, it's essential to be careful and aware of potential scams. Do your research, be cautious, and only invest what you can afford to lose.

Here is a list of notable Indian share market scams with their respective dates:

1. Harshad Mehta Scam (1992): This was one of the first major scams in the Indian stock market, where stockbroker Harshad Mehta manipulated the stock prices using fake bank receipts. The scam caused a loss of around $1.2 billion and led to widespread panic in the market.

2. Ketan Parekh Scam (2001): Stockbroker Ketan Parekh was prosecuted for manipulating the stock prices of several companies and causing a loss of around $1.5 billion. The scam led to stricter regulations on the stock market.

3. NSEL Scam (2013): The National Spot Exchange Limited (NSEL) was a commodity exchange that was closed down in 2013 due to an Rs. 56 billion ($800 million) scam where the company was found to have defaulted on payments to investors.

4. Saradha Group Scam (2013): The Saradha Group, a collective of over 200 companies, was accused of running a Ponzi scheme that defrauded over 1.7 million investors of around Rs. 20 billion ($280 million).

5. PACL Scam (2014): The Pearls Agrotech Corporation Limited (PACL) was accused of running a Ponzi scheme

that defrauded around 5.5 million investors of around Rs. 49,000 crores ($6.8 billion).

6. PMS Scam (2015): The Portfolio Management Services (PMS) scam involved a company called PACL, which was found to have defrauded investors of around Rs. 49,000 crores ($6.8 billion) through its PMS scheme.

7. DHFL Scam (2019): Dewan Housing Finance Limited (DHFL) was accused of diverting funds worth Rs. 31,000 crores ($4.3 billion) and causing a loss to thousands of investors.

8. PMC Bank Scam (2019): The scam involving the collapse of the Punjab and Maharashtra Cooperative (PMC) Bank caused panic among depositors and resulted in a loss of Rs. 4,355 crores ($600 million) to depositors.

5

Ponzi Scheme and its Scams

One kind of scam is a Ponzi scheme that tricks people into giving their money to the scammer. The scammer promises to invest the money and grow it. Still, instead, they use the money from new investors to pay the old investors. It's like a never-ending chain that keeps going as long as new people put in their money.

Think of a Ponzi scheme as a game of musical chairs. The scammer starts by telling people they'll make a lot of money if they give him their cash. As long as enough new players are joining the game and giving the scammer money, he can keep paying the older players and make it look like everyone is winning. But eventually, the music stops, and there aren't enough new players to keep the game going. That's when the scammer runs away with the money and leaves everyone else holding an empty bag.

So, the key to avoiding a Ponzi scheme is to be careful and do your research before giving anyone your money. And if something seems too good to be true, it probably is!

The term "Ponzi scheme" originated from Charles Ponzi, an Italian businessman who immigrated to the United States in the early 20th century. In 1920, Ponzi began promoting a scheme in which he promised investors a 50% return on their investment within 45 days. Ponzi claimed that he could generate these returns by buying and selling international postal coupons, which could be exchanged for stamps at a profit. However, Ponzi was not actually buying and selling coupons; instead, it was using the money from new customers/investors to pay returns to existing customers/investors. The scheme collapsed in 1920 when Ponzi could not bear the returns he had promised.

Ponzi schemes can take many forms, but they all share the same basic structure. The scheme operator will typically promise investors a high rate of return on their investment, often with little or no risk. To entice investors, the operator may provide false information about the scheme's investments, returns, or the operator's qualifications. Once investors have invested their money, the operator will use the funds from new investors to pay returns to existing investors. This makes the investment appear successful and encourages new investors to join the scheme.

Ponzi schemes can be challenging to detect, as the operator will often provide false information about the scheme's investments, returns, or the operator's qualifications. However, there are some red flags that investors should be aware of:

- **High returns with slight or no risk:** Ponzi schemes often promise high returns with slight or no risk. Remember that all investments come with some level of risk.
- **Pressure to invest quickly:** Ponzi schemes often pressure investors to invest speedily and may discourage investors from taking the time to research the investment.
- **Lack of transparency:** Ponzi schemes may need more clarity and may be unwilling to provide detailed information about the scheme's investments or returns.
- **No legal documents:** Ponzi schemes may need the proper legal documents and registration, and the operator may need appropriate qualifications.

Here are some notable examples of Ponzi scheme scams:

1. **The Bernard L. Madoff Scandal:** In 2008, it was revealed that Bernard L. Madoff, a well-known investment adviser, had been operating a Ponzi scheme for decades. The system collapsed when Madoff could no longer pay out the returns that he had promised, causing a loss of around $65 billion to investors.

2. **The Allen Stanford Scandal:** In 2009, it was revealed that Robert Allen Stanford, the chairman of the Stanford Financial Group, had been operating a Ponzi scheme. The scheme collapsed when Stanford could no longer pay out the returns that he had promised, causing a loss of around $7 billion to investors.

3. **The Saradha Group Scandal:** In 2013, the Saradha Group, a conglomerate of over 200 companies, collapsed, causing a loss of around Rs. 24,000 crores to 1.7 million depositors. The company had collected money from small investors, promising high investment returns. Still, in reality, the returns were paid out of the contributions of new investors rather than from actual profits.

6

Real Estate and its Scams

Real estate refers to the buying, selling, and renting properties such as houses, apartments, commercial buildings, and land. In India, the real estate market is vast and complex. It can be a great investment opportunity if you do it right.

When buying or renting a property in India, the initial step is to figure out what you're looking for. Do you want a house, an apartment, a commercial building, or a piece of land? Do you have a specific location in mind? What are your budget and timeline? Once you have these answers, you can start looking for properties that match your criteria.

In India, there are many different ways to find properties. You can look online, where many websites and portals list properties for sale or rent. You can also work with a real estate agent to help you find properties that match your needs and negotiate the best deal for you.

Now, just like in any market, some scams and shady dealings can happen in the real estate market. One common scam is a fake property scam, where a scammer poses as a property owner or agent and offers you a phony property for sale or rent. They might ask you for money upfront as a "security deposit" or "processing fee" and then disappear with your cash.

Another scam is called a substandard property scam, where a scammer sells you a property in much worse condition than they promised. For example, they might sell you a property that's supposed to be brand new, but when you arrive, you find that it's falling apart and needs a lot of repairs.

So, how can you protect yourself from real estate scams in India? Firstly, always do your research and verify the credentials of the property owner or agent before making any payments. Secondly, inspect the property thoroughly before making a purchase, and never rely on just the photos you see online. And finally, consider working with a lawyer specializing in real estate who can help you navigate the complex process and ensure that everything is legal and above board.

Overall, the real estate market in India can be a great investment opportunity. Still, it's essential to be careful and aware of potential scams. Do your research, be cautious, and always take the time to understand the process before making any decisions.

Here Is A List For You:

1. **Fake property scams:** Scammers pose as property owners or agents and offer artificial properties for sale or rent, asking for money upfront as a "security deposit" or "processing fee" and then disappearing with the money.
2. **Substandard property scams:** Scammers sell properties in much worse condition than promised, for example, a property that is supposed to be brand new but is actually falling apart and needs a lot of repairs.
3. **Undervalued property scams:** Scammers sell properties for much less than they are worth, either because they hide defects or use false appraisal reports.

4. **Overpriced property scams:** Scammers sell properties for much more than they are worth, either by inflating the property's value or lying about its features and benefits.

5. **Unapproved land scams:** Scammers sell land not approved for development or in a protected area, and the buyer eventually discovers that they cannot build or use the ground as they intended.

6. **Misrepresented property scams:** Scammers deliberately give false information about a property, for example, its location, size, ownership, or zoning.

7. **Unregistered property scams:** Scammers sell properties not registered with the local government. The buyer eventually discovers they do not have legal ownership of the property.

8. **Unauthorized development scams:** Scammers develop properties without the necessary permits and approvals. The buyer discovers that the property is illegal and cannot be used or sold.

9. **Phantom property scams:** Scammers offer properties for sale or rent that do not exist and ask for money upfront as a "security deposit" or "processing fee."

10. **Inheritance scams:** Scammers claim that a property is available for sale or rent because the owner has passed away and left no heirs and ask for money upfront as a "security deposit" or "processing fee."

11. **Fraudulent mortgage scams:** Scammers offer fraudulent mortgages with attractive terms, but the buyer eventually discovers that the mortgage is not actual and they cannot make payments.

12. **Advance fee scams:** Scammers ask for an advance fee, such as a "brokerage fee" or "tax fee," to complete a real estate transaction and then disappear with the money.

13. **Time-share scams:** Scammers offer time-shares in attractive destinations, but the buyer eventually discovers that the time-share needs to be more accurate or as advertised.

14. **False investment scams:** Scammers offer fraudulent real estate investment opportunities, such as "pre-construction deals" or "property flipping," and ask for money upfront as a "security deposit" or "investment."

15. **Property management scams:** Scammers offer property management services. Eventually, the property owner discovers that the scammers must manage the property properly and keep the rent for themselves.

7

Physical Gold/Silver and Its Scams

In India, physical gold and silver jewelry are regulated by several government agencies and organizations, including the following:

Bureau of Indian Standards (BIS): BIS sets standards for gold and silver jewelry in India, such as hallmarking and quality standards, to ensure that customers receive high-quality products.

Department of Consumer Affairs (DCA): DCA is responsible for consumer protection and ensuring that customers receive fair treatment when purchasing gold and silver jewelry.

Ministry of Mines: The Ministry of Mines is responsible for regulating precious metals, including gold and silver, and implementing policies and programs related to mining and producing these metals.

Gem / Jewelry Export Promotion Council (GJEPC): GJEPC is a government-supported organization that promotes the export of gem and jewelry products, including gold and silver jewelry, from India.

Indian Bullion and Jewelers Association (IBJA): The IBJA is a trade organization that defends the rights of bullion and jewelry dealers in India and informs and counsels its members on matters pertaining to the gold and silver jewelry industry.

These agencies and organizations work together to ensure that the gold and silver jewelry trade in India is transparent, fair, and of high-quality and to protect the rights of customers who purchase gold and silver jewelry in India.

I want to explain the fake gold and silver argument in Indian jewelry. You have two 2000 rupees, one you received from "Bank A" and another one received by "Bank B"; you trust both because it's authorized by the Reserve Bank of India (RBI). Now, when it comes to physical gold and silver, see if it has "hallmarking" or not. If yes, then gold and silver are genuine, irrespective of the jeweler. The risk is minimal when you purchase gold and silver. Always compare the actual weight of silver and the wastage, comparing the charge costs from other stores, and you find the best price to purchase. I buy 22 (916) and 24 (999) carat gold. For silver, I am buying 999 coins and bars. I don't purchase silver ornaments. Silver ornaments contain 92.5% silver and 7.5% other metals. If you buy silver ornaments, stay within 92.5%, and ensure it's marked.

List of scams that happen worldwide:

- **Counterfeit gold and silver scams:** Scammers sell fake gold or silver products, such as coins, bars, or jewelry, and the buyer eventually discovers that they are not real.
- **Misrepresented gold and silver scams:** Scammers deliberately give false information about the quality, weight, or purity of gold or silver products, and the buyer pays more than the products are worth.
- **Overpriced gold and silver scams:** Scammers sell gold or silver products for much more than they are worth, either by inflating the value of the products or by lying about their features and benefits.

- **Gold and silver investment scams:** Scammers offer false gold or silver investment opportunities, such as "rare coin collections" or "limited edition bars," and ask for money upfront as a "security deposit" or "investment."
- **Gold and silver storage scams:** Scammers offer to store gold or silver for a fee, but eventually, the customer discovers that their products have been lost or stolen.
- **Gold and silver lease scams:** Scammers offer to lease gold or silver to customers. Eventually, the customer discovers that the lease needs to be more accurate or that the scammers have sold their products without permission.
- **Gold and silver bullion scams:** Scammers sell gold or silver bullion. Still, the customer eventually discovers that the bullion is not authentic or is not as advertised.
- **Gold and silver coin scams:** Scammers sell gold or silver coins. Still, the customer eventually discovers that the coins are not genuine or are not as advertised.

Chapter Thirteen

People Brainwashed

1

Ancient Civilization

People have been brainwashed by entertainment throughout history, and it's fascinating to look back and see how different civilizations used this powerful tool to control the masses. Ancient civilizations were no exception; they utilized entertainment to spread propaganda, shape public opinion, and maintain power. Let's dive into some examples to see how this was done.

In Ancient Greece, theater performances were an integral part of life and served as a means of education and entertainment. Playwrights often included political messages in their plays, which were acted out in front of thousands of people. For example, playwright Aeschylus was known for his critiques of the government and its policies, which he included in his plays. In this way, the theater was used to spread political messages and influence public opinion.

Epic poems were also used for political propaganda in Ancient Greece. Homer's "Iliad" and "Odyssey" were widely read and taught, and they contained moral and political messages that shaped the values and beliefs of the people. For example, the "Iliad" celebrated the virtues of honor, courage, and loyalty, which were essential values in Ancient Greece.

In Ancient Rome, gladiatorial games and chariot races were used to distract citizens from political unrest and reinforce the ruling class's power. The games were held in the Colosseum, a massive arena that could seat tens of thousands of people. The games were often brutal and violent, but they were also wildly popular, and citizens flocked to the Colosseum to watch them. The games were used to keep the masses distracted from political and social problems and reinforce the ruling class's power.

Ancient China was another civilization that used entertainment to control the masses. Emperors used great cultural performances, such as opera and acrobatics, to distract citizens from political and social problems and maintain their power. These performances were often accompanied by elaborate feasts, and the emperor would use the occasion to distribute gifts and rewards to his loyal followers. In this way, entertainment was used to reinforce the emperor's power and to shape public opinion.

In short:

- **Ancient Greece:** Theater performances and epic poems were used to spread political propaganda and influence public opinion.
- **Ancient Rome:** Gladiatorial games and chariot races were used to distract citizens from political unrest and reinforce the ruling class's power.
- **Ancient China:** Emperors used great cultural performances, such as opera and acrobatics, to distract citizens from political and social problems and maintain their power.

Overall, entertainment has been a powerful tool for brainwashing and manipulating public opinion throughout history. Ancient civilizations used theater, epic poems, gladiatorial games, and cultural performances to spread propaganda, shape values and beliefs, and maintain power. While these methods may seem primitive by today's standards, they were highly effective in their time. They demonstrated entertainment's enduring ability to influence the masses.

2

Modern Civilization

In modern times, the power of entertainment to brainwash people is as strong as ever. Today, entertainment is a multi-billion dollar industry that reaches billions of people worldwide through various media platforms, including television, movies, music, video games, and social media. These forms of entertainment can be highly influential, shaping our beliefs, values, and attitudes in subtle and profound ways. Let's look at how this is done in modern civilization.

Television is one of the most powerful forms of entertainment in modern times. It can reach billions of people worldwide. TV shows and commercials can be highly influential, as they often depict lifestyles, values, and beliefs that are desirable to the viewer. For example, advertisements for luxury cars and designer clothing are designed to make us feel like we need these things to be happy, successful, or attractive. In this way, television can shape our desires and beliefs about what is essential in life.

Movies are another form of entertainment that can be highly influential. They can be used to depict political, social, and cultural issues in a way that shapes public opinion. For example, Hollywood has a long history of portraying American values and ideals in its movies, which can profoundly impact how people view themselves and the world around them. Similarly, movies that depict violence and conflict can shape our beliefs about the nature of violence and its role in society.

Music is another form of entertainment that has the power to shape our beliefs and values. Music can evoke strong emotions and memories, and it can be used to spread messages and influence public opinion. For example, protest songs have a long history of being used to express political opinions and call for change. Similarly, popular music can shape our attitudes toward specific social issues, such as gender, race, and sexuality.

Video games are another new form of entertainment, but they have already proven highly influential. Video games can shape our beliefs about violence, teamwork, and cooperation. For example, military-themed video games can shape our attitudes toward war and conflict, and sports games can shape our beliefs about collaboration and competition.

Social media is a relatively new form of entertainment, but it has already profoundly impacted our society. Social media, like Facebook, Twitter, and Instagram, allow us to connect with people worldwide. They can be used to spread messages and influence public opinion. For example, social media can promote political campaigns, shape public opinion on controversial issues, and spread misinformation.

Overall, entertainment in modern civilization is highly influential. It can shape our beliefs, values, and attitudes subtly and profoundly. Whether it's through television, movies, music, video games, or social media, entertainment can reach billions of people worldwide and shape how we view ourselves and the world around us. It's essential to be mindful of the messages being conveyed through entertainment and be critical of how they may influence our beliefs and values.

3

Avoid Being Influenced

How you can avoid being positively influenced by entertainment:

Be mindful of your choices: Take some time to think about the entertainment you consume and the messages it conveys. You might choose to seek out forms of entertainment that promote positive values and beliefs that align with your own.

Mix things up: Try to diversify the forms of entertainment you consume so you can get a well-rounded perspective on the world. This might include reading books, listening to podcasts, or watching documentaries in addition to your regular TV shows and movies.

Seek out alternative perspectives: When you come across a piece of entertainment that doesn't align with your values or beliefs, try to find alternative sources that offer a different perspective. This can help you to broaden your horizons and challenge your assumptions.

Engage With Others: Talk to Your Friends and Family About the Entertainment You Enjoy and Why You Like It. This Can Help You Gain New Insights and Perspectives and Identify the Messages Being Conveyed in Different Forms of Entertainment.

Reflect on your values: Take some time to reflect on your values and beliefs, and be mindful of how the entertainment you consume influences your thoughts and actions. Suppose you feel that a particular form of entertainment has a negative impact. In that case, limiting your exposure or seeking alternative forms of entertainment that align more closely with your values might be a good idea.

Create Your Own Entertainment: Try to Create Your Own Forms of Entertainment, Such As Writing, Painting, or Playing Music. This Can Be a Fantastic Way to Express Yourself and Make Positive Messages That Align With Your Values and Beliefs.

Stay Informed: Stay Informed About Current Events and Issues so You Can Better Understand the Context and Implications of the Messages Being Conveyed in Entertainment.

Take a break: Sometimes, it's helpful to take a break from all forms of entertainment and focus on finding the things that bring you joy and peace. This could mean spending time outdoors, practicing mindfulness, or connecting with friends and family.

Use Your Voice: If You Come Across a Piece of Entertainment Promoting Messages You Disagree With, Don't Be Afraid to Speak Out and Share Your Perspective. This Can Help to Raise Awareness and to Promote Positive Change.

Have fun! Remember that entertainment is meant to be enjoyed, so make sure to have fun and let yourself relax and be entertained. The most important thing is to find forms of entertainment that bring joy and positivity into your life.

Chapter Fourteen

Fiat Currency Influence

1

Inflation & Deflation

Both **inflation** and Deflation can significantly impact the economy and people's lives, so it's essential to understand how it works.

Inflation and Deflation are terms used to describe changes in the general price level of goods and services in an economy over some time.

Inflation is when prices go up, meaning currency value goes down. Imagine you had 10 rupees to buy a candy bar yesterday, but today that same candy bar costs 11 rupees. This is an example of **inflation**.

Deflation is just the opposite. It's when prices go down, meaning currency value goes up. Let's say that a candy bar from before now costs 9 rupees instead of 11 rupees. This is an example of Deflation.

Think of it this way: imagine you have a big basket of fruits and veggies you want to sell. If the demand for your basket goes up, and there's not enough fruit and veggies to go around, you might have to raise the price of your basket so that you can still make a profit. This is similar to what happens in the economy with **inflation**.

Imagine that there's suddenly a massive crop of fruits and veggies, and there's more than enough to go around. With all the extra supplies, you might have to lower the price of your basket so that people will still buy it. This is similar to what happens in the economy with Deflation.

Inflation is like when you go to the store, and suddenly everything is more expensive than before. That 1 rupee candy bar you used to buy is now 1.50 rupee. This means that the money in your pocket is less than it used to be.

Deflation is like going to the store, and suddenly, everything is cheaper than before. That 1.50 rupee candy bar is now 1 rupee. This means that the currency in your pocket is worth more than it buys.

When more and more currency expands, the economy will end up with **inflation**.

When more and more fiat currency expands, the economy will end up with hyperinflation.

When more and more currency shrinks in, the economy will end up with Deflation.

2

Governments & Individuals

Debt is a double-edged sword that can be helpful and harmful, depending on its use. On the one hand, debt can provide people and governments with access to money. They might not otherwise have, allowing them to make investments or cover expenses they couldn't afford. On the other hand, debt can also be incredibly dangerous and lead to severe consequences if not managed correctly.

Too much debt can lead to financial stress and difficulty making ends meet for individuals. When people have high debt levels, keeping up with monthly payments and interest charges can be challenging, resulting in missed costs and late fees. Over time, this can damage their credit score and make it more difficult for them to access credit in the future.

In some cases, high debt levels can also lead to bankruptcy, which can have long-lasting consequences on a person's financial stability and future. For example, bankruptcy can stay on a person's credit report for up to 10 years and directly impact accessing credit, renting an apartment, or even getting a job.

Similarly, for governments, too much debt can also have serious consequences. Governments with high levels of debt may have to spend a considerable portion of their budget on debt repayment, leaving less money for other essential programs and initiatives.

This can lead to education, health care, and infrastructure cuts, negatively impacting citizens' well-being.

High government debt levels can lead to a financial crisis in extreme cases. The government cannot repay its debts and is forced to seek a bailout from international organizations such as the International Monetary Fund (IMF). This can result in austerity measures, such as tax increases and spending cuts, hurting citizens' standards and the living economy.

Overall, debt can be a helpful tool for individuals and governments. Still, it's essential to use it wisely and avoid too much debt. By being mindful of their debt levels and ensuring they have a solid plan for repaying their debts. Individuals and governments can avoid the dangers of debt and achieve financial stability and success.

Government debt leads to:

1. **Economic instability:** High government debt levels can lead to financial instability and make it difficult for the government to respond to future economic shocks.
2. **Reduced public services:** A significant portion of the government's budget may be dedicated to debt repayment, leaving less money for critical public services like education, health care, and infrastructure.
3. **Difficulty attracting investment:** A government with high debt levels may need to be more attractive to investors. They may be concerned about the government's ability to repay its debts.
4. **Currency devaluation:** A government's debt can lead to a loss of economic confidence. This results in an underestimation of the currency and increased inflation.

5. **Risk of default:** If a government cannot repay its debts. It may be at risk of default, which can have severe consequences for the economy and the well-being of citizens.

Individuals' debt leads to:

1. **Financial stress:** High debt levels can lead to increased financial stress and difficulty making ends meet, hurting overall well-being.
2. **Missed payments and late fees:** When individuals have too much debt. It can be burdensome to keep up with monthly payments and interest charges, leading to cut costs and late fees that can damage their credit score.
3. **Decreased credit score:** High debt and missed payments can harm an individual's credit score, making it more difficult for them to access credit in the future.
4. **Bankruptcy:** In some cases, high debt levels can lead to bankruptcy, which can have long-lasting consequences on an individual's financial stability and future.
5. **Difficulty accessing credit:** A low credit score can make it more difficult for individuals to get a job.

3

Bailouts

A bailout is when a government or organization provides financial support to another government, company, or individual to help them overcome financial difficulties. This can take the form of a loan, an investment, or other forms of financial assistance.

Think of it like lending a helping hand to someone in need. The goal is to prevent the recipient from facing more serious financial problems, such as bankruptcy or collapse, and help them get back on their feet.

Bailouts are often used when the recipient is considered too big or important to fail, as their financial problems could have a broader impact on the economy or society. While bailouts can be a lifeline for those in need, they can also raise questions about fairness and whether taxpayers' money should be used to help those in financial distress.

It's important to note that creating money through bailouts can positively and negatively affect the economy. At the same time, bailouts can provide much-needed financial assistance to those in need. They can also contribute to **inflation** and increase the government's debt levels, which can have long-term economic consequences.

Bailouts Print New Currency:

1. **Central bank lending:** The central bank can lend money directly to the government or financial institutions in financial distress. The government or financial institutions can use this money to assist needy individuals or companies.

2. **Printing of currency:** The government can also print new money to fund the bailout. This increases the supply of money in the economy, which can contribute to **inflation** and reduce the currency's value.

3. **Deficit financing:** The government can finance the bailout by borrowing money from the central bank or other sources, such as bonds or loans. This increases the government's debt levels and may contribute to **inflation** if the government cannot repay the debt.

4. **Monetary policy:** The central bank can also use monetary policy. To influence the availability of money in the economy. For example, the central bank can lower interest rates, which makes it easier for individuals and companies to access credit and can stimulate economic activity.

Risks of Bailouts:

1. **Cost to taxpayers:** Bailouts can be expensive and may involve the use of public funds, which can be a burden on taxpayers.

2. **Lack of accountability:** The recipient of a bailout may need to be held accountable for their financial problems, which can be frustrating for taxpayers who are footing the bill.

3. **Encouraging risky behavior:** Bailouts can create a sense of security and make recipients feel less responsible for their financial situation. Leading them to make difficult decisions in the future.

4. **Unfairness:** Bailouts can raise questions about fairness. Some may believe that the recipients should be held responsible for their financial problems rather than receive assistance from taxpayers.

5. **Potential for dependency:** Bailouts can create a sense of dependence, where recipients become reliant on financial assistance and don't take steps to improve their financial situation.

Bailouts India, Sri Lanka, and Pakistan:

India:

1. 2020 COVID-19 Pandemic Bailout: In 2020, the Indian government provided financial assistance to individuals, companies, and institutions facing financial difficulties due to the COVID-19 pandemic. The bailout amount was estimated to be hundreds of billions of rupees.

Sri Lanka:

1. 2016 Debt Restructuring Bailout: In 2016, Sri Lanka received a financial bailout from the International Monetary Fund to restructure its debt and address its fiscal problems. The bailout amount was estimated to be in the billions of US dollars.

Pakistan:

1. 2013 International Monetary Fund Bailout: In 2013, Pakistan received a financial bailout from the

International Monetary Fund to address its fiscal problems. The bailout amount was estimated to be in the billions of US dollars.

2. 2020 COVID-19 Pandemic Bailout: In 2020, the Pakistani government provided financial assistance to individuals, companies, and institutions facing financial difficulties due to the COVID-19 pandemic. The bailout amount was estimated to be hundreds of billions of rupees.

Bailouts in Other Countries:

1. 2008 US Financial Crisis Bailout: In 2008, the US government provided a financial bailout to several large banks and financial institutions facing financial difficulties in the global financial crisis. The amount of the bailout was estimated to be trillions of dollars.

2. 2012 European Sovereign Debt Crisis Bailout: During the European sovereign debt crisis of 2012, several European countries, including Greece, Ireland, Portugal, and Spain, received financial assistance from the European Union and the International Monetary Fund to address their debt issues. The bailout amount varied depending on the country, but it was estimated to be in billions of euros.

3. 2008 UK Banking Bailout: In 2008, the UK government provided a financial bailout to several large banks, the Royal Bank of Scotland and Lloyds Banking Group, to prevent a collapse of the financial system in the wake of the global financial crisis. The bailout amount was estimated to be hundreds of billions of pounds.

4. 2013 Cyprus Banking Bailout: In 2013, the European Union and the International Monetary Fund provided a financial bailout to the Cypriot banking system to address its financial difficulties. The bailout amount was estimated to be billions of euros.

5. 2020 COVID-19 Pandemic Bailouts: In response to the COVID-19 pandemic, governments around the world have provided financial assistance to individuals, companies, and institutions that are facing financial difficulties. These bailouts have taken various forms, including direct payments, loan guarantees, and other conditions of financial support. The amounts can vary greatly depending on the country and the specific circumstances.

4

Quantitative Easing

Have you ever heard of quantitative easing before? It might sound like a significant, scary term, but it's a terrific way for central banks.

It all started in 2001 when the Bank of Japan decided to try it. The Japanese economy was going through a rough patch, and they needed a little extra push to get things moving again. So, they started creating new money and using it to buy government bonds and other financial assets. This helped to get more money flowing in the economy and, hopefully, get things growing again.

And you know what? It worked! Other central banks worldwide saw what the Bank of Japan was doing and thought, "Hey, that's a great idea! Let's give it a try too!" So, many central banks now use quantitative easing to help their economies when they need a little extra boost.

So, instead of considering quantitative easing as a big, complicated thing, think of it as a friendly helping hand for the economy. It's a tool that central banks can use to get something to move in the right direction when things get tough. Cool, right?

Quantitative easing sounds fancy, but it's just a way for central banks to help boost the economy. For a while, this might seem like a good idea initially, but it can also lead to problems if not done carefully.

Let's imagine you have a giant piggy bank that you can use to help out when things get tough. This is like what central banks do when they use quantitative easing. They create new money and use it to buy things like government bonds to help get more money flowing into the economy.

But just like with your piggy bank, creating too much new money can lead to problems. For example, if there's a lot more money around, it can make things more expensive. This is called **inflation**, which can make it harder to buy something you need, like food or clothes.

Another problem with quantitative easing is that it can lead to asset price bubbles. Imagine if you started to buy lots of toys, and all of a sudden, everyone thought toys were worth more. This could lead to toy prices increasing, even if they're not worth more. The same can happen with financial assets when central banks buy them using the new money they created.

And, just like with your piggy bank, keeping your interest rates low for too long can make it easier for you to earn a decent return on your savings. This can be tough for people who are relying on their savings to help them in their later years.

Finally, it can lead to a moral hazard when central banks seem like they're always willing to help. This is when people take on more risk, knowing that they'll be protected if things go wrong. Just like if you knew your piggy bank would always bail you out, you might need to be more careful with your spending. This can lead to financial instability, which is never a good thing.

So, while quantitative easing can be a helpful tool, it's essential to use it carefully to avoid these problems. And that's why everyone needs to understand what it is and how it works!

List of some of the critical rounds of quantitative easing conducted by the Reserve Bank of India (RBI), along with the amount of money infused into the financial system:

1. March 2020: The RBI conducted open market operations (OMOs) worth ₹50,000 crores ($6.9 billion) to inject liquidity into the financial system.
2. April 2020: The RBI conducted OMOs worth ₹1 lakh crore ($13.9 billion) to support the financial system.
3. May 2020: The RBI conducted a unique Long-Term Repo Operation (LTRO) of 3 years tenors worth ₹1 lakh crore ($13.9 billion) to provide more long-term liquidity to the financial system.
4. June 2020: The RBI conducted a special targeted long-term repo operation (TLTRO) worth ₹50,000 crores ($6.9 billion) to provide targeted liquidity support to specific sectors of the economy.
5. August 2020: The RBI conducted another round of OMOs worth ₹20,000 crores ($2.8 billion) to inject liquidity into the financial system.

These rounds of quantitative easing by the RBI were aimed at providing support to the Indian economy and ensuring the smooth functioning of the financial system in the face of economic challenges posed by the COVID-19 pandemic.

5

Velocity of Currency

Let's dive into the velocity of currency with an easy understanding.

Think about when you last went shopping. You took some money with you and used it to buy the things you needed. Now imagine that every time you spend that money, it gets passed along to the next person who uses it to buy something. This is how the velocity of currency works - money is constantly circulating and used to purchase goods and services.

Let's imagine that you and your friends all have a certain amount of money, and you all decide to save it instead of spending it. In this scenario, the velocity of currency would be low because money is not changing hands as much. On the other hand, if everyone was spending their money freely, the speed of cash would be high.

The velocity of currency can significantly impact the economy as a whole. When money changes hands frequently, people spend freely, businesses sell more, the economy grows, and everyone feels good. On the other hand, when the velocity of currency is low, it can be a sign that people are feeling cautious and holding on to their money, which can lead to a slowdown in economic activity.

Many factors can influence the velocity of currency, such as consumer confidence, interest rates, and credit availability. For example, suppose interest rates are low. In that case, people may be more likely to borrow and spend money, which can increase the velocity of currency. On the other hand, if interest rates are high, people may be more likely to save their money, leading to a lower currency speed.

Overall, the velocity of currency is a fun and exciting concept that can help us understand the economy and how money is changing hands. By tracking the speed of cash, we can get a better idea of how people spend and save their money, which can provide valuable insights into the economy's health.

Here are some examples of the velocity of currency in action:

1. **A thriving economy:** Imagine a city where the local economy is booming, and people feel confident about their financial situation. In this scenario, the velocity of currency is likely to be high as people are spending money freely and frequently. Businesses are selling more, and the overall economy is growing.

2. **A recession:** Now imagine a city where the local economy is in a recession, and people are cautious about spending money. In this scenario, the velocity of currency is likely to be low as people are saving their money and not spending it as much. Businesses are selling less, and the overall economy is slowing down.

3. **A change in interest rates:** Let's say the central bank raises interest rates. In this scenario, the velocity of currency may decrease as people are more likely to save their money instead of spending it. If the central bank

lowers interest rates, the speed of cash may increase as people are more likely to borrow and spend money.

4. **Increased consumer confidence:** Imagine a city with a recent increase in consumer confidence. In this scenario, the velocity of currency is likely to be high as people feel confident about the economy and their financial situation, and they are more likely to spend money.

5. **A natural disaster:** Finally, let's imagine a city hit by a natural disaster. In this scenario, the velocity of currency may decrease as people are more likely to save their money and be cautious about spending it. On the other hand, if there is a large influx of aid and resources, the velocity of currency may increase as people use this money to purchase goods and services.

6

Civilization Investment Plans

During ancient civilizations, people invested in physical assets and had limited investment plans; now, modern society is investing in digital and paper investments with many options and more risk involved, which is bogus.

Ancient Civilizations:

1. **Agricultural Land:** Agricultural land was a popular and secure form of investment in ancient civilizations. People would purchase or lease land to grow crops and raise livestock for food and income. This type of investment provided a steady source of food and income, making it a popular choice for those looking to secure their financial future.

2. **Precious Metals:** Silver and gold were highly valued in ancient times and often used as currency. People would store their wealth in precious metals for safekeeping, as they were seen as a stable and secure investment. Gold and silver were also used as a currency, allowing people to easily trade and exchange wealth.

3. **Trade and Commerce:** Trade and commerce were also important sources of investment in ancient civilizations. People would invest in goods, such as spices, silk, or precious stones, and trade them with other societies to

profit. This investment requires a good understanding of the market and a willingness to take on risk.

Modern Civilizations:

1. **Stocks and Bonds:** In modern times, stocks and bonds are popular investment forms. People can purchase company shares and receive a portion of their profits or buy bonds issued by governments or corporations and receive interest payments. Stocks and bonds provide a way for people to invest in the growth of companies and economies, allowing them to earn substantial returns on their investments.

2. **Real Estate:** Real estate remains a popular form of investment in modern civilizations. People can buy properties, such as houses, apartments, or commercial buildings, and earn money through rent or the appreciation of the property's value. Real estate investment requires a significant amount of capital. Still, it can provide a stable source of income and long-term growth.

3. **Mutual Funds and ETFs:** Mutual funds and Exchange-Traded Funds (ETFs) allow people to invest in a diverse portfolio of stocks, bonds, or other assets. This type of investment can provide a balanced and less risky way to invest in the market, as it spreads risk across multiple purchases rather than relying on a single asset.

4. **Cryptocurrencies:** In recent years, cryptocurrencies, such as Bitcoin, have become a new and exciting form of investment for many people. Cryptocurrencies use blockchain technology to allow for secure and

decentralized transactions. At the same time, this type of investment is still relatively new.

Here's a list of some of the standard bank investment plans available for individuals in India:

1. Fixed Deposits: Fixed deposits are low-risk investments in which the investor deposits money for a fixed term and earns interest at a predetermined rate. They are offered by banks and other financial institutions.

2. Recurring Deposits: Recurring Deposits are similar to fixed deposits, but instead of making a lump sum deposit, the investor makes regular deposits over some time.

3. Public Provident Fund (PPF): PPF is a long-term savings scheme offered by the gov of India. It provides a fixed interest rate and offers investor tax benefits.

4. National Savings Certificate (NSC): NSC is a savings scheme offered by the government of India that provides a fixed interest rate and offers tax benefits to the investor.

5. Sukanya Samriddhi Yojana: Sukanya Samriddhi Yojana is a savings scheme for the girl child offered by the government of India. It provides a fixed interest rate and offers investor tax benefits.

6. Life Insurance Policies: Life insurance policies are offered by life insurance companies and can provide death benefits to the beneficiaries as well as savings and investment opportunities to the policyholder.

7. Unit Linked Insurance Plans (ULIPs): ULIPs are a type of life insurance policy that invests a portion of the premiums in the stock market. They offer both insurance and investment benefits to the policyholder.

8. Mutual Funds: Investment vehicles that pull money from multiple investors to invest in a diversified portfolio of stocks, bonds, and other assets. They are managed by professional fund managers and offer different investment options to suit risk profiles.

9. Equity-Linked Saving Schemes (ELSS): ELSS is a mutual fund that invests primarily in equity-based instruments. They offer the potential for higher returns and are tax-efficient, making them a popular investment option for those looking to save on taxes.

These are some of the standard bank investment plans available for individuals in India. It's essential to consider your personal financial goals and risk tolerance and research the market conditions before making investment decisions.

7

The Income Tax System

The income tax system was manufactured in the United States on July 1, 1862, during the Civil War.

1862, during the Civil War, to help finance the war effort. The US government was facing a significant financial deficit due to the high cost of the war and needed to find a new source of revenue to help fund the military and other expenses. The introduction of an income tax was seen as a way to raise funds from the citizens who were benefiting from the protection provided by the government and the military. The income tax was initially established as a temporary measure but was later made permanent in 1872.

Initially, the income tax system in the United States was designed to target the wealthy. The first income tax law, enacted in 1862, only applied to individuals with taxable income above a certain threshold and taxed them at a rate of 3% on income over that threshold. In 1894, a new law was introduced that taxed a more comprehensive range of payments, including the income of middle-class Americans. Still, this law was later declared unconstitutional by the Supreme Court.

Only by ratifying the 16th Amendment to the US Constitution in 1913 did the income tax become a permanent fixture of the American tax system and be applied to all Americans regardless of income level. Today, the US has a progressive income tax system in which those with higher income levels are taxed at higher rates than those with lower income levels.

The income tax system in India was introduced in 1860 under British colonial rule. Still, it was later replaced by a new approach in 1922. India's current income tax system was introduced in 1961 after India gained independence from Britain.

Initially, The income tax system was designed to target the wealthy. Every average citizen thinks the tax is good as it applies only to the wealthy class. Still, rich people always find a solution. Many wealthy people know how to avoid it legally. But Middle-class people couldn't find the key, and now the central part of income tax incomes are from middle-class society.

8

Government Deficit Spending

Deficit spending by the government can definitely have an impact on us as individual taxpayers. Still, it's not all doom and gloom! We'll look closely at how government deficit spending affects us and explore potential upsides.

Think about when a government spends more money than it receives. It's said to be a deficit. The government may borrow money by issuing bonds or printing more currency to pay for this. Both of these options can have an impact on us as individual taxpayers.

One possible outcome of deficit spending is that we might have to pay higher taxes. This is because the government will need to repay the debt they've taken with interest, which could mean higher taxes for us. But it's essential to remember that this is just one potential outcome. There are many factors at play, and the future is always uncertain!

Another impact of deficit spending is that it can lead to **inflation**. This happens when there's too much money in circulation, and prices start to go up. Our money becomes worth less when prices go up, and we can't buy as much with it. So, it's essential to keep an eye on **inflation** and ensure we save and invest our money wisely.

The government may also reduce the deficit by cutting spending or reducing government benefits. This is called austerity, and it can be tough on us taxpayers. But it's also important to remember that the government is trying to balance the budget and ensure that we can afford the services and programs we rely on.

Despite these challenges, there are also some benefits to deficit spending. For example, government spending can help stimulate the economy and create jobs during tough economic times. This can help get the economy back on track, and when the economy is doing well, we all benefit.

Overall, deficit spending can impact us as individual taxpayers.

Here are a few types of deficit spending that the government may engage in:

1. **Cyclical Deficit:** This deficit spending occurs when the economy is in a recession, and government spending is increased to stimulate growth.
2. **Structural Deficit:** This deficit spending occurs when a government spends more money than it receives, even when the economy is doing well. This can happen because the government has committed to specific programs or spending levels that are difficult to reduce.
3. **Budgetary Deficit:** This is the most common type of deficit spending. It occurs when the government spends more money than it takes each year.
4. **Trade Deficit:** This type of deficit spending occurs when a country imports more goods and services than it exports. This can impact the government's budget because it affects the revenue it has to spend.

5. **Monetary Deficit:** This deficit spending occurs when the government creates more money than it takes in. This can lead to **Inflation** and other economic problems, so it's essential to be mindful of how the government manages the money supply.

By understanding these different types of deficit spending, we can better understand how the government's spending decisions can impact us as taxpayers.

9

Credit Cards

You are responsible for creating new money in the economy, which may lead to **inflation**.

The idea of a credit card was born in the United States back in 1950, and it quickly revolutionized the way we make purchases. The first credit card was introduced by Diners Club and was explicitly designed for use at restaurants. However, as many people started using it for other assets, the concept of a credit card became increasingly popular.

Credit cards are a convenient tool we use daily to make purchases, book a trip, or even get cash. But have you ever thought about the magic that happens when you swipe your credit card? It's not just a simple transaction. It actually has the power to create new money in our economy!

Think about it like this: when you take out a credit card, the bank gives you a loan in the form of a line of credit. This means you can use that credit to make purchases or withdraw cash and then pay it back with interest. And when you use your credit card to buy something, the money goes straight into the seller's account, just like cash. But here's the thing: money in the seller's history can now be used to make their own purchases, and those purchases can then be used to pay for other things, and so on.

This money cycle moving from one person to another creates new economic money.

This process is called credit creation and is not just limited to credit cards. Banks can also create new money through other loans, like personal loans, mortgages, and business loans. However, credit cards are especially effective because they allow for easy and fast access to credit, which means people can spend more and boost the economy.

It's important to remember that great power comes with great responsibility. Like how you need to pay back a credit card loan, too much credit creation can lead to **inflation**, which is when prices go up because there's too much money chasing too few goods and services.

And suppose people are unable to pay back their loans. In that case, the banks may face financial losses, which can impact the stability of the banking system and the economy.

In the end, credit cards are a convenient tool that has the power to create new money and boost the economy. But it's up to us to use them wisely and only borrow what we can afford to pay back. I buy gold and silver using credit cards.

Using credit cards that you should keep in mind:

1. **High-Interest Rates:** Credit cards often come with higher interest rates than other forms of credit, such as personal loans or mortgages. When you don't pay your bill balance in full each month, you could pay a lot in interest charges over time.

2. **Fees:** Credit cards can also come with various fees, such as annual fees, late payment fees, and over-the-limit fees.

It's essential to read the terms and conditions of your credit card carefully to understand what fees you might be charged.

3. **The temptation to Spend More:** Credit cards make it easy to spend money, even if you don't have it. This can be tempting, but it can also lead to overspending and getting into debt.

4. **Risk of Fraud:** Credit cards are a common target for fraudsters, as they provide an easy way to access someone's finances. It's essential to keep your credit card information safe and monitor your account regularly to detect any unauthorized transactions.

5. **Impact on Credit Score:** How you use your credit card can impact your credit score, which measures your creditworthiness. Late payments, high balances, and maxing out your credit limit can all negatively impact your credit score.

10

Home Loan

Home loans, or mortgages as we commonly call them, have been around long ago! The earliest home loans can be noticed back to ancient Babylon, where they were used to help people purchase land and homes.

Fast forward to the 20th century, and we see the introduction of modern home loans in the United States. In 1934, the government created the Federal Housing Administration (FHA) to help more people achieve their dream of owning a home.

Home loans were introduced in India in the late 1970s and early 1980s. At that time, the government of India and state-owned financial institutions, such as the Housing Development Finance Corporation (HDFC), began to offer home loans to encourage people to invest in the housing sector.

Yes, home loans can create new money in the economy. When a person takes out a home loan, the bank or financial institution that issues the loan makes new money by adding the loan amount to the borrower's account. You can then use that new cash to purchase a home.

Home loans can create new money in the economy. Still, it's crucial to ensure that this money is used responsibly and sustainably to support economic growth while avoiding negative impacts such as **inflation**.

EMI Enemy is the amount you need to pay each month to repay your home loan. The EMI amount is calculated based on the (P) loan amount, (R) interest rate, and (N) loan tenure (the number of years you will repay the loan).

To calculate the EMI for a 35 lakh rupee home loan in India, you can use an online EMI calculator or use the following formula:

EMI = [P x R x (1+R)^N]/[(1+R)^N-1]

Where:

- P = Loan amount (35 lakh rupees)
- R = Interest rate (expressed as a decimal)
- N = Loan tenure (in months)

For example, if you take a home loan of 35 lakh rupees at an interest rate of 8% per annum for 20 years (240 months), your

EMI would be approximately 33,667 rupees per month. This is a rough estimate, and the actual EMI may vary based on the loan terms and conditions offered by the bank or financial institution.

It's essential to remember that the EMI is just one aspect of the cost of a home loan. There may also be other charges, such as processing fees, legal fees, and stamp duty, that you will need to pay when taking out a home loan. Make sure to carefully review all the costs and terms associated with a home loan before deciding to ensure that you are fully informed and aware of all the responsibilities and obligations involved.

Suppose you choose to buy a home with a home loan. In that case, you will typically need to make a down payment of 10-20% of the purchase price and repay the loan in monthly installments over 15-30 years. One advantage of this option is that you can get into a home sooner than if you were to save up the total purchase price and enjoy the benefits of home ownership right away. Additionally, the interest paid on a home loan is often tax deductible, which can help to reduce your overall tax bill.

Choose to save up to buy a home outright. You will avoid the cost and obligation of a home loan, including interest payments, fees, and other costs associated with a home loan. Additionally, you will have the peace of mind of knowing that you own your home outright and are not carrying any debt. This can be a particularly appealing option if you are risk-averse and prefer to avoid the uncertainty associated with taking on debt.

Ultimately, deciding whether to buy a home with a home loan or to save up and buy a home outright is personal.

Not paying your home loan can have some severe consequences. Here are a few risks to keep in mind:

1. **A lower credit score:** If you miss payments, your credit score could take a hit, making it more complicated and more expensive to get credit in the future.
2. **Foreclosure:** Your lender could take your home if you don't make payments, resulting in the loss of your equity in the property.
3. **Legal action:** Your lender may take legal steps to recover the amount owed, including wage garnishment or seizure of assets.
4. **Higher interest and fees:** Late fees, increased interest rates, and accelerated loan balances are all possible if you miss several payments.
5. **Repossession:** Your lender may take physical possession of the property and sell it to recover the amount owed.
6. **The strain on finances:** You'll need to pay the outstanding balance, plus interest and fees, which can strain your finances.

11

Student Loan

"The Soviet Union now has a greater number of scientists and engineers in the combined category than the United States. And it is producing graduates in these fields at a much faster rate."

- On November 13, 1957, President Eisenhower

The Sputnik satellite in 1957 Soviet Union prompted criticism of the American education system for its perceived lack of emphasis on science, technology, engineering, and mathematics (STEM) education. The U.S. was seen as lagging behind the Soviet Union regarding technological capabilities and innovation.

The National Defense Education Act of 1958 was enacted in response to the launch of the Soviet Union's Sputnik satellite in 1957. The NDEA was designed to improve the quality of education in the U.S. focusing on science, technology, engineering, and mathematics (STEM) education. The act provided federal funding for STEM education, research, and language and area studies programs. It also offered low-interest loans for college students, focusing on students studying STEM subjects. The NDEA was a crucial step in the U.S. response to the Sputnik shock and played a significant role in shaping the American education system and preparing future generations of scientists and engineers.

Criticism started in the American education system, and it is now worldwide.

1. National Defense Education Act (NDEA) of 1958: Provided federal funding for STEM education, language and area studies programs, and low-interest loans for college students.
2. Higher Education Act (HEA) of 1965: An established framework for several student loan programs, grants, work-study programs, and tax benefits for higher education expenses.
3. Direct Loan Program, 1993: Consolidated federal student loan programs into a single program.
4. College Cost Reduction and Access Act, 2007: Reduced interest rates, increased grant funding, and expanded loan forgiveness programs.
5. Health Care and Education Reconciliation Act, 2010: Further reduced interest rates and expanded income-driven repayment options.

When India Started

1. Indian Education Loan Scheme, 1987: Provided financial assistance to low-income students for higher education in India.
2. Sarva Shiksha Abhiyan, 2001: Government initiative to provide free and compulsory education, including scholarships and student loans.
3. Vidya Lakshmi Portal, 2015: One-stop platform for students to access various educational loan schemes offered by banks in India.
4. Education Loan Subsidy Scheme, 2016: Provided interest subsidies on educational loans for economically weaker sections and socially disadvantaged groups.
5. Pradhan Mantri Fasal Bima Yojana, 2018: Provided insurance coverage and financial support to educate farmers' children.

In the United States, the total student loan debt was estimated to be over $1.6 trillion as of 2021, which significantly impacts the country's economy. In India, the student loan market is rapidly growing. Still, the exact amount of student loan debt is private.

Let us talk about money's role here.

Education loans do not create new money. They are a form of borrowing. Education loans are taken out by students or their families to pay for the costs of higher education, such as tuition, fees, room and board, books, and other expenses. When a student or family takes out a loan, they borrow money from a lender, such as a bank, credit union, or government agency. The borrower then pays back the loan, with interest, over time.

Governments can provide education loans through various programs and initiatives, such as student loan programs, grants, scholarships, and financial aid packages. The funding for these programs can come from a variety of sources, including:

1. **Tax revenues:** Governments can use tax revenues to fund education loan programs and other initiatives to promote access to education.

2. **Bond issuances:** Governments can issue bonds, which are debt securities that raise funds for specific projects or initiatives, including education loan programs.

3. **Allocations from the national budget:** Governments can allocate funds from their national budgets to education loan programs and other initiatives aimed at promoting access to education.

4. **Private-public partnerships:** Governments can partner with private companies and organizations to provide students with education loans and other forms of financial aid.

The funding sources for government education loan programs can vary by country and may include a combination of the above sources.

Student education loan debt can be a financial burden for many students and their families, and there are several risks associated with taking out student loans, including:

1. **High levels of debt:** Student loans often result in high levels of debt that can take many years to pay off. This can lead to financial stress and make it difficult for individuals to afford other essential expenses such as housing, food, and transportation.

2. **Difficulty finding employment:** The high levels of student loan debt can make it difficult for graduates to find a job, as they may need more funds for job-seeking activities, such as relocation and other expenses.

3. **Limited earning potential:** Students who take out student loans to finance their education may find that their earning potential could be improved by the high levels of debt they carry.

4. **Risk of default:** If students cannot make their student loan payments, they risk defaulting on their loans, which can have serious consequences, including wage garnishment, damaged credit, and legal action.

5. **Limited flexibility:** Many student loans have strict repayment terms and conditions, which can limit the flexibility of borrowers to make changes to their repayment plans or adjust their payments to meet their changing financial needs.

Compound Interest

The formula for compound interest is as follows:

A = P(1 + r/n)^(nt)

where:

A = the future value of the investment/loan, including interest
P = the principal investment/loan amount
r = the annual interest rate (decimal)
n = the number of times that interest is compounded per year
t = the number of years the money is invested/borrowed for

The formula for compound interest can be used to calculate the growth of an investment or the total amount to be repaid on a loan, taking into account the effect of compounding over time.

Compound Interest Formula

Compound Interest In Fiat Paper Rupee/Currency:

Did Einstein say compound interest is the eighth wonder of the world?

Quote, There is no proof that Albert Einstein ever declared that compound interest is the eighth wonder of the world, according to the investigator. However, most copywriters and marketing specialists traditionally adored using well-known figures to highlight particular phrases that assisted organizations in boosting their sales.

Compound interest is a great way to make your paper currency grow over time.

Here's a simple example: Let's say you kept ₹100 in a savings account that earns 5% interest per year. After the first year, you would have made ₹5 in interest, bringing your balance up to ₹105.

Now, in the second year, you would earn interest not only on your original ₹100 but also on the ₹5 in interest you made in the first year. So, instead of earning just ₹5 in interest like you did the first year, you would earn ₹5.25 (5% of ₹105).

Each year you continue to leave your money in the account, your interest will be calculated based on a larger and larger balance, allowing your money to grow even faster. And that's the magic of compound interest!

So, the longer you leave your money in an account that earns compound interest, the more it can grow, making it a powerful tool for building wealth over time.

Compound Interest In Physical Gold/Silver:

Invest in physical gold or silver and hold it for an extended period. You may see the value of your investment growth due to factors such as increasing demand, rising **inflation**, or a weakened currency. In this case, you could earn compound interest-like returns on your gold investment. Our paper money is always weakened reason is its fiat currency, gold and silver price will be higher even during Deflation.

Compound Interest when Fiat Rupee/Currency Fails:

When a currency is having a tough time and might not be worth as much as it used to be, it can be confusing and stressful for people with investments. The value of assets, including those earning compound interest, can be impacted by factors like market changes and economic instability.

If you have money in investments tied to a struggling currency, it can be tough to watch the value of your assets decrease. It can make it hard to see your money grow through compound interest.

However, some people look at alternative investments, like physical gold and silver, to protect their money and watch it grow, even during tough times with a currency. For example, choose to invest in gold and hold onto it for a while. In that case, the value of your investment may increase as demand for a stable and valuable asset grows or if other factors like **inflation** or a weak currency are present.

It's important to remember that investing in physical gold, or any other investment, is not a guarantee. There is some level of risk involved. Considering what you're comfortable with and your investment goals would be best.

Chapter Fifteen

Famine

1

Defining Famine

A famine is a situation where there is a severe shortage of food, leading to widespread hunger, malnutrition, and even death. It has numerous potential causes, such as natural disasters, war, and economic instability.

Think about a time when you were starving and couldn't access food for an extended period. That's a tiny glimpse of what a famine can feel like for entire communities. It's a challenging and scary situation and can lead to widespread suffering.

But even during a famine, there are always glimmers of hope. People congregate to help one another and seek solutions. Aid organizations and governments often provide food and support, and communities band together to help their neighbors.

Famines result in widespread hunger and malnutrition and can lead to other serious consequences, such as disease outbreaks, displacement, and even conflict. They can have a devastating impact on families and communities, especially those who are already vulnerable and marginalized.

It's important to remember that famines are preventable and that they can be avoided with adequate resources, planning, and preparation. This includes investing in sustainable agriculture, improving access to food and water, and ensuring that communities are strong and resilient in the face of disasters and other shocks.

But when a famine does occur, we must respond quickly and effectively. This means providing food and water, treating malnutrition and other health problems, and supporting people as they work to rebuild their lives.

So, while famines are undoubtedly tricky, they are an opportunity for us to come together and make a positive difference. Whether it's through volunteering, donating, or simply raising awareness, every little bit helps. And by working together, we can help to end famines and build a more just and equitable world for all.

2

The Madras Famine of 1877

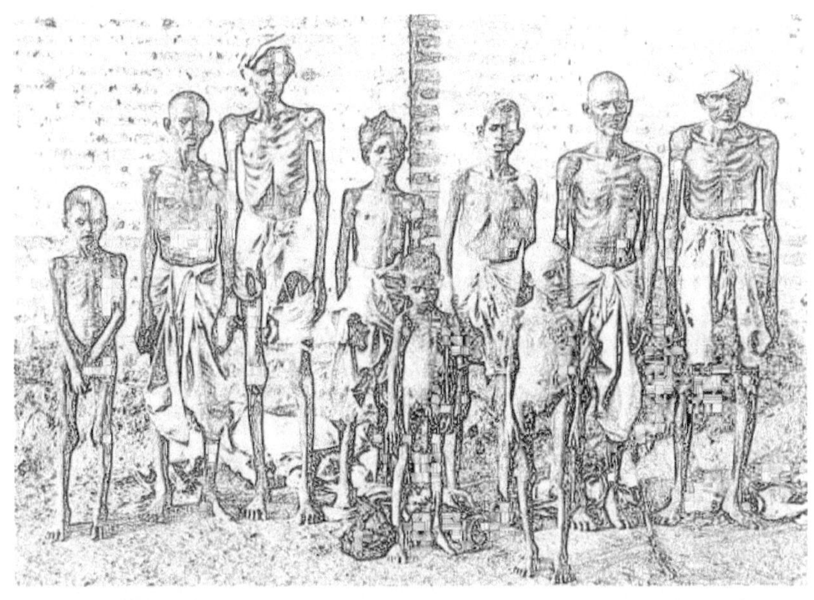

The Madras Presidency was a bustling and vibrant region at the time, with a rich cultural heritage and a thriving agricultural economy. But all of that changed with the onset of the famine. For reasons of survival and employment, people were compelled to leave their homes and towns, which resulted in widespread evictions and misery.

The Madras Famine of 1877 was a significant event in the history of India. It was a great time of hardship and suffering for the people of the Madras Presidency, which covered parts of present-day Tamil Nadu, Andhra Pradesh, and Karnataka. The famine was caused by various factors, including drought, disease, and poor harvests.

The drought was particularly severe in 1876, leading to a water shortage for drinking and irrigation. This, combined with a fungal disease that attacked the crops, resulted in a widespread failure of the monsoon harvest. People were forced to rely on stored grain to survive, but with so many people needing food, stocks quickly depleted.

As the situation worsened, food prices and other essentials skyrocketed, making it increasingly difficult for people to survive. Many were forced to sell their possessions and even their children to buy food. People started to die from hunger and disease with no work available and no food to eat.

The British government, which then ruled India, needed to respond to the crisis faster.

Eventually, they took some measures to help, such as importing food and setting up relief camps. Still, these efforts needed to be improved, and it was too late for many people. By the time the rains returned in 1877, it was estimated that nearly 5 million people had died as a result of the famine.

The Madras Famine had far-reaching consequences. It devastated the local economy, and it took many years for the region to fully recover. It also highlighted the need for better infrastructure and planning to mitigate the effects of future droughts and famines.

Today, the Madras Famine serves as a reminder of the importance of preparing for and responding to natural disasters and other crises. It is a monument to the resilience of the human spirit in the face of difficulty and a depressing warning of the misery that may occur when governments fail to respond promptly and effectively.

Despite the difficult circumstances, many inspiring stories of bravery and resilience emerged from the famine. People came together to support one another, sharing what little they had and working to provide aid to those in need. This spirit of community and cooperation is something that we can all learn from, even today.

It's important to remember that famines like the 1877 Madras famine didn't just affect the people of India. They had a ripple effect, touching the lives of countless others around the world. That's why it's so important to pay attention to the needs of those in crisis and to do what we can to help.

So, the next time you hear about the 1877 Madras famine, take a moment to reflect on the power of human kindness and resilience. Remember the lessons we can learn from this event, and think about what we can do to make an effort in today's world. Whether volunteering at a local food bank or simply reaching out to a friend in need, every act of kindness counts.

Overall, the 1877 Madras famine was a tragedy that caused immense suffering and loss of life. However, it also taught us important lessons about the need to be better prepared for natural disasters and other crises. Let us remember the lessons of the Madras Famine and work to ensure that such a tragedy is never repeated.

Some of the most critical famines in history are listed below:

- The Great Irish Famine (1845-1852)
- The Bengal Famine (1943)
- The Ethiopian Famine (1983-1985)
- The North Korean Famine (1995-1998)
- The Sahel Famine (1968-1974)
- The Sudan Famine (1998)
- The Ukraine Famine (1932-1933)
- The Bengal Famine (1770)
- The 1877 Madras Famine (1876-1878)
- The Great Chinese Famine (1959-1961)
- The Somalia Famine (2010-2012)
- The Horn of Africa Famine (2011-2012)
- The Soviet Famine (1921-1922)
- The Great Leap Forward Famine (1958-1961)
- The Vietnamese Famine (1945-1946)
- The Malawi Famine (2002)
- The Zimbabwe Famine (2002-2003)
- The Bangladesh Famine (1974)
- The Mozambique Famine (1991-1992)
- The Niger Famine (2005)

3

COVID-19 Famine

The COVID-19 pandemic has created previously unheard-of difficulties, challenges, and hardships, including the COVID-19 famine. A famine is a widespread food shortage leading to widespread malnutrition, starvation, and death. The COVID-19 famine results from the pandemic's impact on food systems, including supply chain disruptions, reduced agricultural productivity, and loss of income for farmers and food producers.

The pandemic has disrupted global food supply chains, leading to shortages of essential food items and higher prices. This has been particularly devastating for countries that rely on imports to meet their food needs. In addition, the pandemic has led to reduced agricultural productivity as workers fall ill, are quarantined, or must stay home to care for sick family members. This has resulted in reduced crop yields and lower-quality crops.

The COVID-19 famine has also significantly impacted the livelihoods of farmers and food producers. Many have lost their income due to reduced demand for their products, and others have been unable to get the products they need to market due to disruptions in transportation and logistics. This has left many communities in a state of food insecurity and at risk of malnutrition and starvation.

Despite the challenges, there have been efforts to address the COVID famine and ensure that communities can access the food they need. Many organizations and governments have increased food aid and assistance programs. They are working to restore and strengthen food supply chains. In addition, some communities are turning to sustainable agriculture practices, such as regenerative agriculture, to increase local food production and reduce their dependence on imports.

While the COVID-19 famine presents a significant challenge, it is also an opportunity to rethink and rebuild our food systems to be more resilient, sustainable, and equitable. By supporting local and sustainable agriculture, reducing waste, and ensuring that everyone has access to healthy and nutritious food, we can create a food system that is better equipped to withstand future shocks and crises.

Overall, the COVID-19 famine reminds us of the importance of food security and the critical role that food systems play in our lives. By working together to support farmers, food producers, and communities in need, we can help mitigate the pandemic's impact and build a more resilient and sustainable food system for the future.

4

Protect Your Family

Protecting your family from famine can seem daunting. Still, with some planning and preparation, you can ensure their safety and well-being. Here are some steps to consider:

1. Keep some physical gold and silver with you during the famine; this will help you to convert to your needs.

2. Stock up on non-perishable food items: Building a stock of non-perishable food items is one of the crucial things you can do to prepare for famine. This includes canned goods, dried goods, and other food items with long shelf life. Store these items in a cool, dry place and rotate your stock regularly to ensure freshness.

3. Start a vegetable garden: Growing your own food is a beautiful way to ensure that you and your family have a steady supply of fresh produce. You can start a vegetable garden in your backyard or on a windowsill if you live in an apartment. This not only provides you with fresh produce but also helps you save money and have control over what you eat.

4. Store clean water: Clean water is essential for survival, so have bottled water or fill large containers with fresh water that can be stored for an extended period. Consider investing in a water filtration system to ensure the water you keep is safe to drink.

5. Make a plan: Famines can happen quickly, so it's essential to have a plan in place. Ensure each family member knows what to do and where to go in an emergency. This may include a designated meeting place, evacuation routes, and a plan for how you will communicate with each other.

6. Stay informed: Keeping track of any warnings or updates about potential famines in your area is critical to staying safe. Stay informed by monitoring the news, local weather reports, and social media.

7. Support your community: Helping others in need can make a big difference in times of famine. Consider volunteering with local organizations or donating food and supplies to those struggling.

8. Diversify your food sources: In the event of a famine, food may become scarce and expensive. Consider diversifying your food sources by hunting, fishing, or foraging for wild edibles.

9. Be mindful of your food consumption: During a famine, it's essential to be aware of your food consumption. Avoid wasting food, and try to make the most of what you have. This may include eating smaller portions or cooking nutritious and filling meals.

Remember, preparation is vital! Taking these steps can protect your family and ensure their safety during a famine.

Chapter Sixteen

Spend More Money

1

The Art of Making Textiles in Ancient Times

Making textiles was a proper art form in ancient civilizations and an integral part of their daily lives. People relied on natural resources, like wool from sheep and flax from plants, to create their own cloth.

The process of making textiles was a long and intricate one. First, the fibers had to be spun into thread, which required patience and a skilled hand. Then, the line was woven into fabric on a loom, a labor-intensive process that took skill and precision.

Once the fabric was woven, it was time for the fun part: dyeing! Using natural pigments. The cloth was transformed into vibrant and beautiful pieces that reflected the culture and traditions of the ancient civilization.

Textiles were a cherished part of ancient life. They were used for clothing, as well as for trade and religious ceremonies. The creation of textiles was a source of pride and was seen as a proper form of artistic expression.

And my love for textiles was not limited to just making them. It was also about wearing and using them. People took great care to maintain the beauty and longevity of their textiles, often repairing and mending them when needed.

Furthermore, textiles played an essential role in shaping the economy of ancient civilizations. They were used as a currency and for trade with other cultures. This made textiles a valuable commodity and helped to solidify their place as an essential part of daily life.

In ancient civilizations like Egypt, the cloth was highly valued and was often used as a form of payment for goods and services. The highest quality linen was especially prized and used for important events like religious ceremonies and even in mummifying loved ones.

In ancient times, the creation of textiles was not just a practical pursuit but a cultural one. Materials allowed people to express themselves, tell their stories, and connect with their community. They were an essential part of the cultural fabric of ancient civilizations.

In short, textiles were a beloved and essential part of ancient life. From their creation to their use, they played a central role in shaping ancient civilizations' culture, economy, and daily life. Today, we continue to be inspired by the beauty and ingenuity of textiles from ancient times, and I honor their place in history by keeping the art of textile-making alive.

Textiles were considered a valuable commodity in Ancient Greece and Rome and were often traded for other goods. Silk was a luxurious item and was usually reserved for the wealthy.

Overall, each step required skill and patience, from spinning the fibers to dyeing the cloth. The results were beautiful and functional pieces that played a central role in daily life. Whether for clothing, trade, or religious ceremonies, textiles were a cherished part of an ancient civilization.

2

The Industrial Revolution – A Game-Changer for Civilization!

It all started in Britain in the late 1700s.

You may have heard the term "Industrial Revolution" Before, but do you know what it really means and how it changed our world? Buckle Up Because This Period Was One Big, Exciting Adventure!

Back in the day, people made everything by hand. Can you imagine that? Everything from clothes to tools had to be crafted one at a time. But then, all of a sudden, machines started showing up and changing everything! Factories sprang up, jobs were created, and goods began being produced at lightning speed. People flocked to cities for work and a new way of life.

One of the most important things about the Industrial Revolution was all the new gadgets and gizmos that came with it. The spinning jenny, steam power, and power loom, to name a few, made life easier and more efficient. And who doesn't love more efficiency, right? It also meant that goods became cheaper and more accessible to everyone. Hello, shopping spree!

But not everything was sunshine and rainbows during this time. Factory work was hard and often dangerous. People had to work long hours and had little control over their work. But the good news - this led to the rise of workers' rights movements and trade unions, who fought for better working conditions and fair treatment. These movements made a big difference and helped improve many people's lives.

Finally, the Industrial Revolution had a significant impact on our planet. With all the new industries and machines came air and water pollution, soil degradation, and the destruction of natural habitats. But we're intelligent, and we've learned from past mistakes. Now, we're working on reducing our environmental impact and making the world an excellent place for future generations.

Overall, the Industrial Revolution was a huge turning point in our history. It changed the way we live, work, and play. While it brought about some challenges, it also opened up a world of possibilities. So next time you put on a t-shirt, hop on a train, or turn on a light, take a moment to appreciate the incredible impact this time had on our world!

3

Can Make Us Spend More Money

Let's Choose A Textile Industry!

The textile industry, including the fast fashion companies, has dramatically impacted how we spend our money in the 21st century. With the constant influx of new styles and trends, it's easy to feel the pressure to keep up with the latest fashions. However, this pressure can lead to overspending and buying items that we don't really need or need to be of better quality.

One of the biggest challenges of the textile industry is the cycle of overproduction and overconsumption. Companies are constantly producing new items at a rapid pace, encouraging us to buy more and more clothes. And when these clothes go out of style, we throw them away and buy even more. This cycle can be hard to break and can lead to waste.

Another challenge is that some companies use misleading marketing tactics to promote their products. They may claim that the clothes are of high quality or ethically made when they are often poorly made and last only a short time. This can make us think we are getting a good deal when spending more money on low-quality items.

And finally, the pressure to keep up with the latest fashion trends can lead us to prioritize fashion over comfort and practicality. We may buy clothes that look good but are uncomfortable or not suited to our lifestyle. This can make us overspend and have a closet full of clothes we don't enjoy wearing.

Overall, the textile industry can significantly impact our spending habits. By being mindful of the cycle of overproduction and overconsumption, being cautious of misleading marketing tactics, and prioritizing comfort and practicality, we can make more informed decisions about what we buy and avoid overspending. Remember, buying what we need and love is always essential rather than just following the latest fashion trends.

Chapter Seventeen

Gold & Silver

1

It is Money

Many people make the judgment, believing that they do not need to physically own their precious metals. Either they can better leverage their position by purchasing mining stocks or judge the paper or digital gold they hold as good as gold. As previously stated, that is sickening thinking.

1. **It has a history:** Silver and gold have been the only investments that have succeeded for the past 5,000 years. They are movable goods with inherent value. Thus their purchasing power will never be zero.

2. **Independent:** Financial assets like gold and silver can be private and independent of the financial system. Even real estate needs to transfer title through the financial system. Silver and gold do not.

3. **Asset:** Assets are rare financial assets that are not a liability to someone else. Stocks, bonds, and derivatives such as futures and ETFs depend on the issuer's or counterparty's performance. Even cash has value only if the government issuing it performs well. A nation's currency also fails if its government does. Silver and gold are infallible.

4. **Tax:** Gold & silver don't require yearly tax. They might be entirely owned. Real estate is one thing you can never

truly own; if you doubt this, try to skip your property tax for a few years.

5. **Investments:** Gold & Silver are investments that rise in times of economic turmoil, conflict, terrorism, and disaster because they are safe havens.

6. **Trust:** Physical gold has a long history of being a store of value, and its value is not dependent on any central authority. On the other hand, fiat currency's value mainly relies on the trust people have in the issuing government and central bank.

7. **Durability:** Physical gold is a durable metal used for thousands of years. Unlike fiat money, It has a long shelf life and doesn't rust or deteriorate.

8. **Recognizability:** Physical gold is widely recognized as a store of value and medium of exchange, making it a globally accepted form of money. Fiat currency, while widely used, may not be recognized or taken in all parts of the world.

9. **Density Value:** They are dense in value. Accordingly, unlike copper or gasoline, a tiny amount of gold or silver provides enormous purchasing power.

10. **Actual Value:** The worth of every single gram of gold & silver & SILVER is the same. An expert is needed for every diamond or collector coin because they need help defining the value.

Physical gold and silver have value because they are real money.

2

Carat Calculation

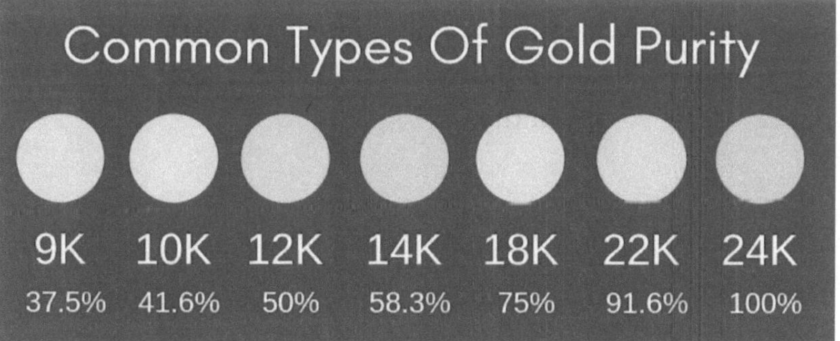

Calculating the carat weight of gold is actually pretty simple. Carat is a measurement used to describe the weight of gold, and one carat is equal to 0.2 grams, or 200 milligrams.

To figure out the carat weight of your gold, you need to know 2 things: the importance of the piece in grams and its gold purity, usually expressed in karats.

Let's say you bought gold weighing 10 grams, and its gold purity is 18 karats (18K). Here's how you would calculate its carat weight:

First, you would divide the gold purity by 24, the total number of karats in pure gold. So, 18 divided by 24 would be 0.75.

Next, you would multiply the weight of the piece in grams by the result you got in the previous step. So 10 grams x 0.75 would be 7.5.

And voila! The carat weight of your gold would be 7.5.

This means you are not purchasing 10 grams of gold when you purchase a piece of jewelry. You are actually purchasing only 7.5 grams of gold.

Silver jewelry 925 is known as sterling silver. It is the most common alloy to manufacture silver jewelry and other acceptable silver items. The silver purity levels generally accepted 99.9% purity – 999. 92.5% purity – 925.

3

Complex to Manufacture

Manufacturing gold and silver is a complex process that involves several stages, requires specialized equipment and skilled workers, and can be time-consuming and resource-intensive.

Fiat currency is relatively straightforward compared to precious metals like gold and silver. It involves a printing process that uses specialized equipment and inks, which can be done relatively quickly and inexpensively.

Here is a comparison of the manufacturing of gold and fiat currency:

Gold:

1. Mining: Gold is extracted from the Earth through mining operations.
2. Refining: The extracted gold is refined to remove impurities and achieve a higher purity level.
3. Fabrication: Refined gold is fabricated into coins, bars, jewelry, or other forms for investment or trade purposes.

Fiat Currency:

1. Printing: The physical currency is printed by the government's central bank or mint.

2. Minting: Coins are minted by the government's central bank or mint.
3. Distribution: The currency is then distributed to banks, financial institutions, and other authorized entities for circulation.

It's worth noting that the creation of digital fiat currency also involves the same central bank issuing and distributing cash through digital means.

Both gold and fiat currency are subject to government regulations and oversight. Still, they differ in terms of their intrinsic value and the backing of the currency.

Gold has been used for thousands of years and has an inherent value based on its scarcity and industrial use. Fiat currency is a legal tender backed by the government issuing it.

Gold is Lord Shiva's Money.

Gold is God's Money.

Silver is a little brother of God's Money.

4

Central Banks Buying Gold

Why are central banks holding the gold if gold is not money? They know gold is money.

Central banks buying gold has become a trend in recent years, with many institutions adding to their gold reserves to diversify their portfolios and protect against economic uncertainty. It will explore why central banks invest in gold and what factors have led to this trend.

One of the main reasons central banks buy gold is to diversify their foreign exchange reserves. This means that central banks are looking to hold a mix of assets, such as gold, currencies, and government bonds, rather than relying solely on one type of asset. A diverse portfolio helps central banks reduce their exposure to economic and political risk and ensures they have access to a range of assets they can use to support their economies.

Another reason central banks buy gold is to hedge against **inflation**. Gold has historically held its value well, even during economic instability and currency devaluation. This makes it an attractive option for central banks, as they seek to protect the value of their foreign exchange reserves from the eroding effects of **inflation**.

Central banks are also buying gold to protect against geopolitical risk. In times of political uncertainty, gold can provide a safe haven for central banks and help protect against the potential for financial instability.

Additionally, the increasing demand for gold from emerging economies, such as China and India, has put upward pressure on gold prices. This has made gold an attractive option for central banks looking to invest in a rapidly growing market.

Here's a list of countries with the largest gold reserves, in no particular order:

1. United States: The United States holds the most significant amount of gold in the world, with over 8,000 tons in its reserves.
2. Germany: Germany is the second largest holder of gold, with over 3,400 tons in its reserves.
3. Italy: Italy holds over 2,450 tons of gold, making it the third largest holder in the world.
4. France: France has over 2,440 tons of gold in its reserves, ranking it as one of the largest holders in the world.
5. Russia: Russia's gold reserves have grown in recent years and currently stand at over 2,300 tons.
6. China: China's gold reserves have also been growing rapidly and now stand at over 1,900 tons.
7. Switzerland: Switzerland is known for its strong banking industry and has over 1,040 tons of gold reserves.
8. Japan: Japan holds over 765 tons of gold in its reserves, making it one of the largest holders in Asia.
9. United States Federal Reserve: The United States Federal Reserve holds the most significant amount of gold globally, with over 8,000 tons in its reserves.

10. Deutsche Bundesbank: The Deutsche Bundesbank, Germany's central bank, is the second largest holder of gold, with over 3,400 tons in its reserves.

11. Bank of Italy: The Bank of Italy holds over 2,450 tons of gold, making it the third largest holder in the world.

12. Banque de France: Banque de France has over 2,440 tons of gold in its reserves, ranking it as one of the largest holders in the world.

13. Bank of Russia: The Bank of Russia's gold reserves have been growing in recent years and currently stand at over 2,300 tons.

14. People's Bank of China: The People's Bank of China's gold reserves have also been growing rapidly and now stand at over 1,900 tons.

15. Swiss National Bank: The Swiss National Bank is known for its strong banking industry and has over 1,040 tons of gold reserves.

16. Bank of Japan: The Bank of Japan holds over 765 tons of gold in its reserves, making it one of the largest holders in Asia.

Yes, India also has a significant amount of gold in its reserves. The Reserve Bank of India holds over 560 tons of gold, making it one of the largest holders in the world.

India has a long-standing cultural affinity for gold, and its central bank's precious metal holdings reflect this. By holding gold in its foreign exchange reserves, the Reserve Bank of India is helping to support the stability and resilience of the Indian economy and protect against economic uncertainty.

The Reserve Bank of India has recently been increasing its gold holdings to diversify its foreign exchange reserves and reduce dependence on other currencies, such as the US dollar.

This trend reflects a broader trend among central banks worldwide as they seek to protect their economies and ensure financial stability in an increasingly uncertain global economic environment.

5

Price Will Go Up

You may have noticed that gold prices have been rising for quite some time now. Experts predict that the trend will only continue. Many believe that the cost of gold will soar even higher in the coming months and years.

So, why is this happening? There are a few reasons. Firstly, gold is considered a haven asset when the economy is shaky. Many investors are turning to gold to protect their riches because the globe is experiencing many difficulties.

Additionally, the increasing demand for gold in emerging economies, like China and India, is also driving up the price. As these countries continue to grow and develop, they are buying more and more gold to meet their needs.

So, what does this mean for you? If you're an investor, this could be an excellent opportunity to invest in gold. You could see significant returns on your investment.

1. **Economic Stability**: When the economy is unpredictable, people often turn to gold as a secure investment.
2. **Central Bank Interest:** Many central banks worldwide have been investing in gold, which helps to support its price.

3. **Dollar Value Fluctuations:** The value of the U.S. dollar can impact the price of gold. If the dollar is weaker, the cost of gold may rise.

4. **Inflation Concerns:** If **Inflation** is high, people may choose to invest in gold to protect their money's purchasing power.

5. **Growing Demand from Emerging Markets:** As countries such as China and India continue to grow, their demand for gold also increases, which can boost their prices.

6. **Political Stability:** Gold is often seen as a haven investment during political uncertainty or conflict.

7. **Supply and Availability:** If the collection of gold is limited, for example, due to mining disruptions, it can drive up the price.

8. **Investment Popularity:** An increasing number of people are choosing to invest in gold, which helps drive its price.

9. **Technological Advancements**: Gold and Silver are used in various specialized applications, such as electronics and solar panels, and as the demand for technology grows, so does the need for gold.

10. **Jewelry Industry**: Gold remains a popular choice for jewelry and the demand for gold increases as more jewelry is bought.

11. **Safe Haven Reputation**: With a long history as a haven investment, gold remains a reliable option during economic uncertainty.

12. **Time-Tested Store of Value:** Gold has been used as money and a store of value for centuries and remains a popular choice for preserving wealth.

13. **Historic Price Trends**: Gold has a proven track record of increasing value over time, providing investors confidence.

14. **Portfolio Diversification**: By including gold in their investment portfolios, individuals can help to protect against market fluctuations.

15. **Government Policies:** Government policies and decisions, such as changes in interest rates or currency devaluations, can also affect the price of gold.

16. **Consumer Confidence:** When people are optimistic about the economy, they may choose to invest in other assets instead of gold, which can impact its price.

17. **Natural Disasters:** Natural disasters such as earthquakes or hurricanes can disrupt the supply of gold and cause its price to rise.

18. **Increased Production Costs:** If the cost of producing gold, such as due to rising energy costs, goes up, this can affect its price.

19. **Economic Growth:** As countries grow and develop, they may increase their demand for gold, which can drive its price.

20. **Market Speculation:** Market speculation, or predictions of the price of gold, can also impact its actual cost.

Brighter Future

Do you want to provide a secure and stable future for your family? Investing in physical gold and silver can help you achieve this goal. These precious metals have been valued for centuries for their stability, durability, and ability to retain their value, making them a smart choice for anyone looking to protect their family's financial future. For a bright future, we'll look closely at why investing in physical gold and silver is a wise decision.

The Power of Physical Gold and Silver:

Physical gold and silver have a long history of preserving wealth and stability, even during economic turmoil. These precious metals are not tied to any particular currency or government, making them a more reliable option in uncertainty. When you invest in physical gold and silver, you own a tangible asset that you can hold onto, and that can provide long-term financial security for you and your family.

Physical gold and silver are also in high demand, making them a more durable option than other forms of investment. They are recognized worldwide as a safe haven for wealth, and their value and stability are not affected by market trends or economic fluctuations. This makes them a smart choice for protecting your family's financial future.

Investing is Easy and Accessible:

Investing in physical gold and silver is an intelligent choice for your family's financial future and is easy to do. You can purchase physical gold and silver in various forms, from coins to bars, to suit your investment goals and budget. And because they are in high demand, physical gold and silver are easy to buy and sell, making them accessible to people of all investment levels.

Whether you're just starting out or have years of experience, you can find the right option to suit your investment goals and budget. Many reputable dealers offer a wide range of options. You can even purchase physical gold and silver online for added convenience.

Diversify Your Portfolio:

Investing in physical gold and silver is the best way to diversify your investment portfolio and reduce overall risk. When you mix different investments, you can reduce your exposure to market fluctuations and economic uncertainty. Physical gold and silver are a safe haven for your wealth, providing stability and financial security for you and your family.

Overall, investing in physical gold and silver is a wise choice for anyone looking to provide their family with a secure and stable future. These precious metals are in high demand, easy to buy and sell, and a great way to diversify your investment portfolio. Don't wait. Take control of your family's financial future and build your precious metals portfolio today.

Gods Money Will Protect You

Many of them will say gold is not a good investment. What I found is only gold and silver gave high returns in this century. Gold went up to 25 times in the 1980s, and Silver went up to 40 times in the 1980s.

This time, we have more to expect!!! Do not ask when. I am 100% confident, and I believe it will be more than in the 1980's.

1. Gold Prices (per ounce):

- 1970s: Started around $35 to $40.
- 1980: Jumped to over $800 at one point!
- 1999-2001: Stayed between $250 and $300.
- 2008: Went up to about $1,000 during a big financial crisis.
- 2011: Reached an all-time high of over $1,900 due to economic worries.
- In recent years, the average price has been above $2,000, sometimes hitting over $2,420,

2. Silver Prices (per ounce):

- 1970s: Started around $1.50 to $2.00.
- 1980: Hit a high of over $50!
- 1990s-2000s: Stayed between $4 and $10 mostly.
- 2011: Went up to around $49 along with gold speak.

- In recent years, generally, it has been above $20, sometimes going over $27.52 during market ups and downs.

It is not how much it is worth; it is all about how much you have gold & silver God's money.

Gold & Silver is an anchor not an engine. Stock & Equities are engines that can break down and fail. Gold is what keeps you steady in heavy seas. Invest accordingly. I do agree that a lot of investors don't care about gold & silver. I recently saw a video giving the case, why we shouldn't buy gold & silver. Looking at the comment section on that video there's a lot of people who are not on board with having god's money gold & silver. When the paper money (Fiat Currency) market eventually breaks down if run on physical gold & silver will likely skyrocket. When I think about where to safely invest my money, gold and silver are the first options that come to mind. Why should I buy gold and silver? Why should i/you buy them? To secure your wealth before it's too late. The big banks are moving into gold too. Why did these banks visits shanghai gold exchange? Standard Chartered Group, United Overseas (China), JP Morgan, HSBC, Deutsche, etc.,

Invest in God's Money—Gold and Silver. Buy them physically and feel like a king!

We are Humans! We are One! Earth is One

"Pale Blue Dot" It is Earth, and it is us.

Many people believe that they are living on Earth. Do you think you can live on Earth without the support of the sun, moon, stars, and other planets? We are not only living on this Earth. We are living everywhere. Likewise, as a human, we need to support one another to have a wonderful life.

Have you ever gazed up at the night sky and wondered about our place in the universe? This incredible "Pale Blue Dot" idea might give you a better perspective.

From space, our planet Earth looks like a tiny blue speck, a mere dot in the vast and infinite universe. But to us, it's home! And that's what makes the "Pale Blue Dot" so unique. It reminds us how lucky we are to have this beautiful planet and all the life on it.

The idea of the "Pale Blue Dot" was popularized by the famous astronomer Carl Sagan. He wrote a book about it and talked about how important it is for us to cherish and protect our planet. He believed that despite our differences, we're all part of the same community, and it's up to us to take care of each other and the planet we call home.

Sagan also had some exciting ideas about the future of humanity. He thought that we have the potential to explore the stars and even colonize other planets! But he also warned us to be mindful of our actions and their impact on the Earth.

So, next time you look up at the night sky, think about the "Pale Blue Dot" and what it represents. Remember that we're all just temporary residents on this speck of blue. Still, it's up to us to make the most of our time here and create a better future for ourselves and the planet.

Being human is all about showing compassion, empathy, kindness, and understanding toward others. It's what makes us unique and sets us apart from other species. And the good news is, anyone can behave like a human with humanity! Here's how:

1. **Put yourself in someone else's shoes:** Imagine how they might feel and try to understand their perspective. It will help you connect with others on a deeper level.

2. **Spread joy:** A simple smile or compliment can go the best way to brighten someone's day. So, be sure to spread cheer wherever you go!

3. **Say thank you:** Taking a moment to express gratitude for the things you have in life can make you feel happier and more appreciative.

4. **Listen with your heart:** When someone is talking to you, listen to what they say. It shows that you care and can help build strong relationships.

5. **Give a helping hand:** Whether volunteering, donating to a cause, or just being there for a friend in need, there are many ways to help others and make a positive impact.

6. **Treat others with respect:** It doesn't matter who someone is or their beliefs. Everyone deserves respect and kindness.

7. **Let go of grudges:** Holding onto anger and bitterness only hurts you in the end. Forgiveness can be tricky, but it's a powerful way to heal relationships and find peace.

8. **Be curious:** Be open to new ideas and perspectives and try to learn something new daily. It can help you grow and make new connections with others.

So, there you have it! By practicing these simple behaviors, you can live a life filled with humanity and positively impact the world around you. Let's make kindness and compassion the norm!

Thank you

Vijayarathinam

Say Thank You!!!

I want to express my gratitude to the entire team at Notion Press for their dedication and hard work on this book, turning my dream into a reality.

He is an invaluable asset to Notion Press, especially with his exceptional marketing skills. He explains the various packages and their offers with remarkable clarity and detail, making him an essential part of my book.

Nishanth. M - Assistant Manager, Notion Press Publishing

I am profoundly grateful for your exceptional guidance throughout the entire publishing process and for being my dedicated point of contact until the book is published. Your support and expertise have made this journey incredibly smooth and enjoyable. It has been a truly wonderful experience working with you, and I sincerely appreciate all that you have done.

Neha Thomas - Publishing Manager, Notion Press Publishing